꘎꘎

Survival Strategies for Going Abroad: A Guide for People with Disabilities

By Laura Hershey

꘎꘎

Mobility International USA
National Clearinghouse on Disability and Exchange
PO Box 10767
Eugene, Oregon 97440 USA
Tel/TTY: 541-343-1284
Fax: 541-343-6812
E-mail: clearinghouse@miusa.org
Web: www.miusa.org

The National Clearinghouse on Disability and Exchange (NCDE) is sponsored by the Bureau of Educational and Cultural Affairs of the United States Department of State.

Table of Contents

Chapter Two:
Making Your International Experience Happen

Chapter Three:
Trip Planning

Acknowledgments

Many people played a part in making this book happen. First, much of the credit for this project goes to the people who shared their stories of traveling with a disability. I made extensive use of travelers' written reports, collected by Mobility International USA (MIUSA) in its *A World Awaits You* journals. These provided a wealth of information. I especially appreciate those who granted me interviews—Rachael Abbott, Rosangela Berman-Beiler, Mary Lou Breslin, Susan Brown, Judi Chamberlin, Alicia Contreras, Tanis Doe, Don Galloway, Frank Hernandez, Harriet Johnson, Jenny Kern, Jean Lin, Marta Lukjan, Jean Marchant, Richard Mouzon, Tia Nelis, David Oaks, Jean Parker, Ellen Rubin and Daisy Sipp. Combined, these travelers' narratives, reflections and advice form the heart of this book.

I want to acknowledge the important work that MIUSA has done for over two decades, promoting international exchange participation by people with disabilities. So many individuals (including some of the people profiled in this book) got their first taste of overseas travel, and experienced an unprecedented level of personal growth and confidence, as a direct result of involvement in MIUSA programs. Never content simply to offer its own exchange programs, MIUSA has continuously educated exchange participants and professionals, and advocated for inclusion of people with disabilities in overseas study, service and other exchange opportunities. Susan Sygall's leadership in this area has made a tremendous difference.

An important MIUSA project, the National Clearinghouse on Disability and Exchange (NCDE), initiated this book. Michele Scheib, NCDE Program Manager, Tracy Scharn, NCDE Project

I

Coordinator, and Pamela Houston, NCDE Public Relations Coordinator, provided guidance, editorial feedback, encouragement, material and numerous contacts as this book was being researched and written. Editorial suggestions were also provided by Susan Sygall, NCDE Project Director/MIUSA Executive Director.

Special thanks are also due to David Levin, Senior Program Manager and Diversity Coordinator of the Bureau of Educational and Cultural Affairs of the United States Department of State, for his extensive advice and guidance, and to his Bureau, which sponsors the NCDE and has funded this publication.

In addition, Brett Campbell served as external editor and Lillian Winkler-Rios designed the cover and layout. Thanks to Jennifer Drinen for her hard work and meticulous care in transcribing all the interviews. Additional thanks to Jack Liu for the photograph for Chapter Five, and to the National Aeronautics and Space Administration for the photo of the Earth on the cover.

Finally, I want personally to thank the people who have made my own journeys possible. My parents, Richard and Faye Hershey, passed along a love of travel, helped grow my dreams while encouraging and supporting me all the way, and let me go (with some trepidation) when those dreams lured me overseas. I thank those attendants who have traveled with me—especially Cara Jean Reimann, Clara Hogan, Helen Wright, Jackie Padgett, Kristin Gonzales, Laurilane Gery, Margi Duran, Marybeth Bell, Sharon Quinn, Stacey Koeckeritz and Trish Donahue—for providing personal assistance during trips both grueling and rewarding.

My partner, Robin Stephens, has been my companion in innumerable adventures and I have benefited from her love, her intrepid spirit and her skill at finding low airfares.

Preface

by Susan Sygall
Project Director, National Clearinghouse on Disability and Exchange
Executive Director, Mobility International USA

In my lifetime of international travel, I have found there are few experiences as truly unique and exhilarating as living in another culture and learning about its real, day-to-day life. When one travels on an international exchange, one experiences opportunities that convey the essence of another culture. It's the moments of tasting a home-cooked meal with a homestay family near a medieval village in France, or appreciating the architecture of the ancient ruins of Uxmal in Mexico, sharing a conversation with a farmer in Vietnam, or admiring the local crafts made by an artistry collective in South Africa that remain fixed in my memory. As my personal and professional passions for international exchange have merged over the years, it has given me the greatest pleasure to see the increased inclusion of people with disabilities in all types of international exchange experiences.

Whether you are a Deaf university student enjoying an art history course in Milan, a pediatrician who uses a wheelchair devoting your vacation to working with HIV orphans in Zambia, a person with a hidden disability interning at a bank in Moscow or a high school student who is blind spending a year in Peru, you too can enhance your life through international experience. Simultaneously, you may become a catalyst for changing people's perceptions about who participates in educational abroad experiences.

This book is in many senses a culmination of several years of work by the National Clearinghouse on Disability and Exchange

(NCDE), a project sponsored by the Bureau of Educational and Cultural Affairs of the U.S. Department of State, and administered by Mobility International USA (MIUSA). Our skilled staff and consultants have produced a unique and useful publication specifically for people with disabilities, or those who have disabled friends or family members, or who work with people with disabilities. International exchange professionals who offer programs and opportunities abroad and others interested in international exchange will also find useful insights included here.

Laura Hershey, an experienced traveler with a disability herself, spent many months interviewing people with a variety of experiences and disabilities to gather tips for planning a successful international exchange experience. In this book, you will find information, strategies and resources to help you prepare to study, work, research, volunteer or teach overseas. Chapter One explores topics from choosing a program to disclosing and accommodating your disability. Chapter Two explains how to apply to a program, as well as fundraising and pre-departure planning ideas to make your experience a successful one. Chapter Three addresses issues such as packing, educational accommodations, staying healthy, tips for people with psychiatric disabilities, the pros and cons of traveling with service dogs, and working as part of a group or team. Chapter Four looks at logistical issues such as getting to your destination, transportation, safety and moving between work, school and home in another country, as well as the topic of cultural interaction. The last chapter prepares you for returning home after your international exchange experience—learning how to maintain friendships across cultures, gaining insight about the impact of your international experience and sharing your experience with others.

The wide variety of exchange experiences makes it possible to find an opportunity that matches each individual's passion, curiosity, quest for knowledge or desire to make a difference in the world. As a person who uses a wheelchair, I studied Spanish in Salamanca, Spain, and attended graduate school in Brisbane, Australia on a Rotary Scholarship; I have volunteered on a community service project in Finland and offered my services as a consultant in places such as Bosnia and Vietnam. As you read this book, you will see that my story is not unique. People with all types of disabilities are becoming an integral force in this amazing field we call international exchange.

We have only scratched the surface of what is possible to ensure that every person with a disability has the same opportunities as our non-disabled peers. The world needs the often-untapped expertise of people with disabilities—and we need to experience other cultures to increase our global understanding and appreciation so we may be successful in whatever field or profession we choose to follow. And all of us—disabled and nondisabled alike—need to have the same opportunities because international exchange is a life-enhancing experience in and of itself—for everyone.

People with disabilities can look forward to a future of greater accessibility and inclusion wherever we study, live, teach, travel, volunteer or work. It is my hope that this book will have a place in opening new doors and creating new opportunities. Remember, we are part of a great family of people with disabilities and we need to work together to share our experiences and strategies so that those who follow may have a wider and easier path to international exchange experiences.

Introduction

by Laura Hershey

In 1995, I went to the People's Republic of China to attend the Non-Governmental Organizations (NGO) Forum, parallel to the Fourth World Conference on Women. I traveled as part of a loosely organized group of women with and without disabilities. These women, about forty in all, came mostly from the United States, but the group also included women from Canada, Mexico and Nicaragua.

We encountered our first barrier right after landing in Beijing. To get to the terminal, we were told, we must go down either an escalator or a flight of stairs. This news was brought to us by a harried American agent from United Airlines, but the directive came from Chinese immigration authorities. There were elevators, said the agent—but we learned that the one near our arrival gate hadn't worked in two years. A second elevator was located on the other side of immigration control; to get to it, we would have to go all the way around customs, descend in the elevator, and then backtrack 100 yards or so to deal with immigration and customs. The authorities simply would not allow that. Therefore, the officials told us, people in wheelchairs always used the escalator.

We all gathered around to discuss our options. We really had no options, but we acted as if we did—for a while. We decided to ask for a meeting with the officials.

We gathered at the top of the escalator to wait for a reply to our request. People coming in from the next flight had to wiggle themselves and their luggage around us. It was a bit awkward.

Eventually, officials came to speak with us. A few women respectfully voiced their concerns about using the escalator. The officials listened with hard looks on their faces, then gave perfunctory, negative replies.

Each woman now had only to look at her own individual options—stairs or escalator—to decide for herself how to handle this situation. Those with lightweight chairs balanced them carefully, and glided backwards down the escalator. Some women walked down awkwardly, holding onto stronger shoulders for support. Others scooted down one step at a time, on their butts. I let myself be bumped down the stairs, tipped far back on the rear wheels of my wheelchair.

We moved forward, haltingly down the stairs or—terrifyingly— down the escalator. We realized that we were no longer in the United States, and that things were different and challenging for us.

As we went to collect our luggage, digital-light signs greeted us inside the terminal:

WARMLY WELCOME WOMEN DELEGATIONS
FROM ALL OVER THE WORLD

MAY THE FOURTH WORLD CONFERENCE
ON WOMEN BE A BIG SUCCESS

MAY OUR FRIENDSHIP
BE LONG LASTING

During the rest of my three-week stay in China, I encountered more barriers and aggravations; but ultimately, the trip provided more than enough positive experiences to make overcoming the obstacles worth the effort. I attended the first-ever International Symposium on Issues of Women with Disabilities, which drew over 200 disabled activists from dozens of countries, a milestone in disabled women's organizing. I befriended my assigned volunteer, Lucy, a delightful, bright young student from the Beijing Language and Cultural Institute who would eagerly engage in conversation about a variety of topics including Chinese history and American novels.

I even made it to the top of the Great Wall of China, my wheelchair frame gripped by strong men working for tips. Several of my friends took the same route, and we all lined up for a photo. It's a joyous, symbolic snapshot—a group of grinning disabled women, proud of our willingness to take a risk and surmount one of the largest physical barriers we would ever face.

Most exciting of all was the NGO Forum. I was surrounded by thousands of women, from every community on the planet— every nationality, every ethnicity, every religion, every culture, every class, every everything. I saw Japanese women courageously refusing to let the world forget what happened to Hiroshima and Nagasaki. I saw Tibetan women insist bravely on their tiny but visible presence at the Forum. I sang along with Sweet Honey in the Rock, the a capella African-inspired gospel/folk/protest vocal group from Washington, D.C. I watched an English woman mix torn strips of paper and water in a blender, spread the pulp on a screen, and thus make textured paper. I sat on a panel discussing economic justice with a Native American health worker, a prisoners' rights advocate and others. I marched with lesbians, proclaiming pride and the freedom to love.

In Beijing, women taught each other how to organize politically, how to speak up about issues, how to make videos, how to access the Internet. Women forged connections that will live on in short-wave radio broadcasts, exchanges of e-mail, newsletters and mailing lists, stories and poems, and lifelong friendships.

For me, Beijing will stay in my memory as a place of many Great Walls, and many reasons to climb them. The experience expanded my horizons globally.

>·⚓·<

Following Your Dreams

If your dreams, your work or educational goals are urging you overseas, you are probably wondering whether you should follow those urgings. If you decide to take that leap into the cultural unknown, what will you find there? What can you expect from your international experience? What benefits can you expect to gain? What lessons might you learn? What kind of problems should you endeavor to solve, in advance if possible?

The answers to these questions vary widely, depending upon the purpose of the sojourn, the locale, and your personality, philosophy and approach to the journey. There are, however, lessons to be learned from those who have been there, and are happy to tell about it.

That is the purpose of this book—to draw on the wisdom and experiences of people with disabilities who have ventured overseas in pursuit of work, study or other exchange opportunities. They went for different reasons, took with them different sets of needs and skills, faced different kinds of challenges and took advantage of different opportunities. They all came back with new knowledge, experiences and strategies which they have generously shared with other disabled travelers.

As you begin to plan your overseas adventure, probe your own expectations. As a participant in international exchange, how do you see your role? Will you be an ambassador for your country? A teacher, a mentor, a role model? An advocate for social causes? Or a learner, seeking new insights and alternative perspectives?

What obstacles are you likely to face in another country? Will the barriers you face in your own neighborhood at home be magnified? Will you encounter completely new, unforeseen problems? Is it possible that some things will be easier for you in a foreign land than in your own hometown?

To what extent are you willing to adjust your expectations regarding accessibility, accommodations and independence? In the West, civil rights legislation and sophisticated technology make possible a high degree of access and equity. That possibility is not always realized, but people with disabilities have a sound basis for expecting a range of equipment, support services and legal protections. If you are traveling to the United States or another developed country for the first time, are you ready to investigate and navigate these new laws and support systems?

The situation may be quite different in developing countries. In much of the world, few technological solutions are available to people with disabilities. For this reason, many veteran travelers with disabilities emphasize the importance of adaptability and flexibility when venturing into this type of foreign territory. Where access is lacking, personal relationships and/or the kindness of others may represent the best possible barrier removal plan.

That was certainly Anatoli Ilyashov's experience. The historian traveled to Russia as a Fulbright scholar. He wondered how he would manage, given his mobility limitations caused by multiple sclerosis. He walked with a cane, and had to deal with old and inaccessible transportation systems. "The Russian people were great in accommodating me under the adverse conditions they were living in," reports Ilyashov. "They were conscious of my situation and often helped me into buses, trams and trolley cars."

In this book, you'll meet many disabled people who have done what you are considering now, in the spirit of seeking new experiences and perspectives. You will hear their stories, both funny and profound. You'll learn how they adapted to foreign environments, how they shared in the cultural richness of their host countries and how their lives were enriched as well. You'll find many practical tips related to access, accommodations, navigation, support and much more. By the time you finish, armed with the knowledge gleaned from other disabled people's journeys, you'll be better equipped to undertake your own journey—which will be uniquely yours—and to make the most of it.

Chapter One

Exploring International Opportunities

Your overseas dreams may be the product of long years of planning and preparation, or they may arise from a flash of inspiration. Either way, as you begin exploring the possibilities that await you in the world, you'll find yourself contemplating your interests and needs, clarifying your goals, studying possible destinations, seeking opportunities, devouring other people's stories and, ultimately, making important decisions. This will be a journey in itself. It may take as long as, or longer than, your actual travels; and it may offer you valuable insights about yourself and your international prospects.

Johana Schwartz, who has cerebral palsy, went through a fairly typical process of envisioning, seeking, finding and choosing an international program. Both scholarly interests and pragmatic disability-related considerations influenced her choices. As a student of the works of James Joyce, Schwartz had wanted to visit Ireland for some time. Her own university did not offer any study abroad opportunities in Ireland, but did refer her to programs available through other institutions. She eventually selected a summer Irish Studies program, operated by New York University, at Dublin's Trinity College. There she found the Irish literature and language courses in which she was interested. Equally important, Schwartz adds, "as an American entity, NYU was subject to the Americans with Disabilities Act." The program largely met her disability-related needs, providing notetakers, a wheelchair-accessible apartment and other necessities.

Other people locate and embark upon their path overseas more quickly, almost instinctively. Marvelena Quesada clearly remembers the day one of her college professors mentioned an upcoming study abroad program at the University of Madrid. Quesada, who is blind and fluent in Spanish, snapped to attention. The departure date was less than a month away. "I had nowhere near enough time to properly prepare," says Quesada, "but I knew that I wanted to go." She filled out the application even though she knew little about Spain "or even whether the program was disability-friendly." It was, mostly, and Quesada (who traveled with her guide dog) was able to learn a great deal about Spanish culture and politics. "The nicest thing about my trip," she adds, "was that I was able to travel independently for the first time. I consider that to be quite an achievement and would recommend this sort of program to anyone with a disability."

Serendipity is nice when it happens—but don't wait for opportunities to seek you out. If you know what you want to do and where you dream of going, actively pursue avenues that will lead you there. "Where do you want to go?" asks Alicia Contreras, who has traveled to Asia, Africa and throughout Latin America in her wheelchair. When you know the answer, Contreras advises, share your goal with others. "Tell every single person you know that you want to go, because someone might know about an opportunity. Spread the word!"

Take the example of Ellen Rubin: Tell everyone about your dream, and sooner or later you may tell someone who can help make it happen. As a Jewish blind woman, Rubin was passionately interested in going to Israel. It was 1967, and Rubin knew that many Israelis had been blinded during the Six-Day War. "I thought it would really be interesting to go there and work with people who were blind," says Rubin. She mentioned her desire to a number of people. "I said it to the right person who had connections," she recalls. A week later, Rubin was offered a grant to visit a rehabilitation center in southern Israel. "I went for three weeks, and I stayed for six years!"

Think about the people you know who might have international connections—family members, friends, colleagues, teachers, community organizations, service organizations, business people or world travelers. Even if you're not particularly close, or have been out of touch for a while, consider reaching out to these individuals. Ask them to meet with you and answer questions about their overseas travel. You may find that people are very willing to take the time to share their stories and ideas, and to answer your queries—especially if you show that you value their thoughts and guidance. These conversations might just lead to further contacts, discoveries of opportunities, maybe even invitations.

Mobility International USA/National Clearinghouse on Disability and Exchange also has an extensive peer network of people with disabilities who have been abroad. Through this peer network you can find others most willing to share their ideas and get you started on your way. For example, Marie Sharp has volunteered at a health clinic in Mexico, taught English in Venezuela and studied in Brazil. As a woman who uses a manual wheelchair, she can share her best tips on getting around, contacts she gathered and strategies for interacting with people from other cultures. (See the Appendix for information on how to request peer contacts.)

5

Develop your own international contacts as well. There are many ways to get to know people from other countries: Join international organizations and read their newsletters. Subscribe to international listservs. Become a host family for foreign visitors or volunteer with exchange programs. Attend international events in your community. Taking these steps will enrich your life and broaden your horizons—and they may also help you find your own way overseas!

You can also research the many international exchange programs that are available. A list of international exchange resources can be found in the Appendix. However, given the wide array of opportunities, this list is far from complete. If you're interested in an international exchange experience, you can also ask around in your local area. You might try contacting organizations you are involved with in your local or broader community, such as philanthropic associations, groups promoting cross-cultural understanding, or social justice groups that work on international issues. Searching the Internet, contacting the study abroad office at local universities, visiting your high school guidance counselor's office and browsing the resources on MIUSA's website (www.miusa.org) provide other good places to begin. If you are a U.S. citizen, you may also want to contact the embassy or consulate of your destination country for information. If you are interested in traveling to the United States from abroad, an excellent informational resource is the EducationUSA advising center in your country's capital city. See the Appendix for further details.

If you are determined to study, volunteer or work abroad, keep looking until you find what you want. Marta Lukjan longed for an international experience, but the kind of program she was seeking was not available at Princeton University where she was an undergraduate. Most of her peers were not interested in international education and were less than supportive of her plan. At the time, she recalls, many students and faculty members questioned why anyone would want to study off-campus, after working so hard to get to Princeton; and with her learning disabilities, she had to work even harder. Lukjan persisted until she found and enrolled in a multi-college study abroad program operated by Butler University. Ultimately, Lukjan actually earned the envy of some of those who had discouraged her. "My room-mates thought I was crazy," she recalls, "but desperately wished they too had planned for such an adventure."

Many different types of opportunities exist for going abroad. The avenue you choose will depend on your situation and goals. In the next section are some of the most common ways of having an international experience.

Types of International Exchange Programs

There are many organizations that arrange exchanges for individuals from different countries. Some of these programs specialize in specific regions, populations or exchange types. For example, there are international exchange programs designed primarily for young people, educators, residents of sister cities, political activists or farmers. You can go abroad to intern, study, volunteer, teach, consult, learn a language or participate in professional development activities. Some exchange programs emphasize learning about topics such as human rights, public health, art history, gender studies, literature or many other topics; others focus on foreign languages and country or area studies. And most programs will help you gain cross-cultural understanding. An international exchange experience can last for a few weeks, or a full year or more, and any length in between.

Short-Term Delegations and Exchanges

If you don't have a long period of time available for an exchange program, consider short-term exchanges, which span most of the above-mentioned exchange types. Some of these exchange programs are highly structured, involving a busy daily schedule of activities and a focused agenda. Jean Parker, a radio journalist who is blind, went to Latin America twice with two different exchange programs. Parker usually prefers traveling alone rather than with a group, but she found these two sojourns valuable because they offered "a way to gain access to people I wanted to talk to," she says. She joined a delegation to Central America, sponsored by the Center for Global Education at Augsburg College. "At that time, there were wars and conflicts going on there," says Parker. "The purpose of those trips was to get a better understanding of those conflicts and the U.S.' role in them." Parker also went to the border area of Mexico and the United States with a group called Border Links to learn about immigration, the impact of globalization and other issues. They talked to both liberals and conservatives alike, going to the land reform offices and government representatives. "That was an educational experience," Parker recalls. It gave participants "a better idea of what the issues were from people on various sides of things."

Getting that much education and information required a tightly structured itinerary packed with field trips and meetings. If that's not your style, there are other programs that are more relaxed, allowing participants more free time to explore the local culture on their own, at a slower pace. Consider which style suits you best when you are seeking and choosing an exchange program.

Jean Marchant, who has multiple sclerosis (MS), advises people who have limited stamina to seriously think about the pace of an exchange. "If you're going to be in one place, that's one thing," says Marchant. However, she traveled to Germany with a Mobility International USA (MIUSA) exchange that involved a lot of day trips and moving from place to place. Marchant remembers the trip as both enjoyable and illuminating, but it took a toll on her, causing fatigue and increased spasticity. She urges people with MS and similar conditions to "find out about the flexibility of the program, in terms of needing to participate in every activity, and being able to prioritize what is important and what is not beforehand."

Academic Programs

Many universities and nonprofit international exchange organizations offer study abroad programs for college or high school students. These programs usually combine both academic study and cultural experiences. For example, the student will typically attend classes, complete assignments, earn credits and take field trips, while also participating in different cultural activities. Students can go on group programs focused on

Sometimes short exchanges can give you a taste of what overseas travel is like, and provide you with contacts, confidence and skills that will be valuable when you go on a longer exchange later. On the other hand, it can take a lot of energy to plan for a trip of any duration, so you might consider staying longer to really get a feel for the community—especially since you never know when you might get a chance to return.

specific topics like the environment, political science, literature, art or architecture. Some of these group programs allow students who may not know the host country's language to take classes taught in their native language while at the same time studying the language of the host country to improve their proficiency. Other exchanges place students directly into the host university or high school, where they can access the same accommodations and experiences as the host country students.

Students with disabilities have participated in and benefited from an enormous variety of overseas exchange programs, some operated by their own schools, some by other schools or by independent programs. Most of these programs offer a structured experience, complete with academic programming and a living situation that may be a host family placement, apartment or on-campus dormitory housing. Factors such as accessibility features, reasonable accommodations and support services will vary widely from program to program; researching these factors may become an important part of your exploration of overseas exchange possibilities. Equally important will be the program's potential to meet your needs for learning, personal growth and career development.

An international educational program may be the beginning of many exciting opportunities. It certainly was for Karla Rivas, a Guatemalan woman who is blind. Rivas was awarded a Fulbright scholarship to study communications at California State University, Chico. This particular Fulbright Program granted at least two years of undergraduate study in the United States to Central American students selected on the basis of financial need and exceptional academic promise. "It was great news for me, but a hard decision," says Rivas. "I was 22 years old and I had never been outside of my country. Being blind, going away from my family was a difficult decision, but my family was always very supportive of me. They said it was not an opportunity that came into your life every day."

A study abroad program can greatly enrich your academic experiences and provide you with cross-cultural understanding. It can also give you extraordinary opportunities to develop your strength and independence as a disabled person. During her sophomore year as an art major, Elizabeth Castellano decided to explore the possibility of studying overseas, hoping it would offer her new opportunities for development, both as an artist and as a person. Castellano, who has a visual impairment, said, "I believed that a study abroad experience would teach me how to become more independent and give me a greater sense of confidence and personal identity." She learned about a variety of study abroad opportunities from her fellow students, and ultimately chose Lancaster University in England "because of its superior services for people with disabilities and its enclosed (self-contained), rural campus."

As an undergraduate at Princeton University, Marta Lukjan took part in an overseas exchange program at the University of Queensland in Brisbane, Australia. As a result of a childhood brain injury, Lukjan has "a really unusual constellation of strengths and weaknesses" including learning disabilities. "Princeton can be intimidating to those with hidden disabilities," she says. "So I viewed study abroad in slightly different terms than most of my classmates." Feeling somewhat out of step with her Ivy League peers, Lukjan was ready to take risks to expand her horizons. While she knew next to nothing about Australia, she knew she needed to "get out of the pressure cooker" and seek new challenges. She found what she was looking for—Lukjan calls her time in Australia "by far the most memorable semester I had" while working toward her college degree.

Language Programs

If you are interested in learning or teaching a language, there are many options to choose from. Hundreds of language training programs are available worldwide. Some programs are short-term and intensive, while others can last up to a year or more. Many language schools offer the option to stay with a host family, do volunteer work, intern or participate in other activities in addition to attending classes, all of which can enrich your understanding of the language and culture you are studying.

Instead of enrolling in a language training program, you may be interested in teaching your native language in another country. While abroad, you will have the opportunity to immerse yourself in another culture and language, and learn from your students as you teach them your language. Zachary Battles, who is blind, spent two weeks on a group exchange to Ukraine where he and other volunteer teachers helped students learn conversational English skills at the Language Institute in Kiev. He says that the teachers became students as well: "The time spent in the classroom was merely a fraction of the teaching and learning experience for both teachers and students. Teachers must be willing to learn as well as teach, and the team of Americans was certainly willing to experience as well as learn about a different culture."

Whether you decided to enroll in a language school or teach at one, there are many books and other resources written on this topic. See the Appendix for a list of options and resources to explore.

Working Overseas

If you have particular skills or a willingness to learn and a strong desire for an international experience, you may want to apply for jobs overseas. Although overseas employment can be one of the most competitive avenues to living abroad, many opportunities do exist. Short-term work programs are good opportunities for college students or recent graduates who want to live abroad for up to a year and work in the hospitality or tourism industry, national parks, or other types of service or administrative jobs. You may be able to work for a foreign company or organization, depending on your own talents and qualifications, and on the applicable laws such as visa requirements for foreign workers. Other work-type options—paid, volunteer or in exchange for room and board—include freelance jobs, seasonal agricultural work, internships and working as an *au pair* or a language teacher.

When Ellen Rubin arrived in Israel and fell in love with the country, she began looking for work. Eventually she found a job in a rehabilitation center for children. After a couple of years, Rubin returned to the United States to obtain a master's degree in special education, then went back to Israel to help set up a program for children with blindness and/or other disabilities. "Our program was an inclusion program; we trained teachers to work with children in various areas and help them integrate into school," Rubin says.

Some people with disabilities have obtained jobs with companies or organizations based in their home country but doing business overseas. The United States government is a major employer. Don Galloway, who is blind, worked as a Peace Corps country director in Jamaica for three years. A friend told him the Peace Corps was interested in hiring people with disabilities.

Galloway loves to travel and already had overseas experience in Latin America and the Caribbean, so he went for an interview and got the job.

Many employment services and job search websites advertise international jobs. You can also find overseas work opportunities through newspaper advertisements, exchange organizations, trade associations and college employment offices. You may want to pay particular attention to announcements from federal agencies that employ large numbers of people at your country's embassies and consulates abroad, for example. The U.S. Department of State and other foreign affairs agencies are an exciting option to consider, although the process is competitive. Consult the Appendix for some leads on overseas work, volunteer and internship opportunities.

In any kind of job search, however, the best opportunities may come from personal contacts. Ask friends and acquaintances to alert you to jobs in the field and country or region in which you are interested. Seek out and introduce yourself to people who are employed in similar situations. Find local companies doing business in countries where you want to work. The Appendix lists exchange programs that provide work visas and/or can match you with a company or organization with job openings.

When considering job opportunities, take note of different employers' policies regarding workers with disabilities. If the company you're applying to work for is based in the United States, and has more than fifteen employees, it is bound by the requirements of Title I of the Americans with Disabilities Act (ADA). This means it cannot deny you a job for which you are qualified, based solely on your disability; and it must provide you with reasonable accommodations, such as adaptive equipment, interpreting or reading services, to enable you to do your job. This also applies to U.S. businesses or organizations operating overseas. While in the United States or working for a qualifying U.S. company, the ADA covers people with disabilities regardless of citizenship. Other countries may have similar laws.

Consulting Overseas

Working abroad need not depend upon finding a permanent job with one employer. Another option is to do various projects for which you can be paid, under contract to one or more client organizations. As a consultant you can find yourself working with many different people, and enhancing your skills with each new project.

Some people build an entire career on freelance work overseas. As a radio journalist, Jean Parker has traveled all over the world— throughout most of Western Europe, India, South Africa, Mexico and most of Central America. Wherever she goes, Parker records interviews, news and feature reports for broadcast on radio stations including the British Broadcasting Corporation. Parker, who is blind, also operates her own program, Disability Radio World-wide, which can be heard on short-wave radio, and on the Internet at www.independentliving.org/radio. Parker says, "I view disability as a social and political condition," in that it is shaped by the context in which one is living, and is influenced by community attitudes, the physical environment, the economic situation and other social factors. "Because I think of it that way, it has led to an interest in people from other places, particularly other places that I don't know much about." Parker learns of interesting stories and potential interview subjects through her extensive personal and professional networks. She is involved in many associations, including disability groups, Quaker organizations and human rights groups. She is also a ham radio operator, and through this medium she meets many diverse individuals throughout the world. Some of them become news sources, advisers, future tour guides and friends.

Perhaps you are a person who is committed to making the world a better place through organizing, advocacy and/or development efforts. You may have a role to play in working for social or political change in other countries. Many people have traveled abroad in the service of causes such as human rights, environmentalism, peace, women's rights and economic development.

In particular, disability rights advocacy has become a worldwide phenomenon. In virtually every country, disabled people are working together to improve their living and working conditions, rights and opportunities. Some of these disability rights groups look to other countries for networking, advice, resources, training, information and inspiration. If you have been active in organizing and advocating for disability rights, and have developed skills that could be beneficial to people in other countries—or if you want to find out about others' work and bring new ideas and perspectives home to your own country—then you may find opportunities to travel overseas to share your knowledge and learn from others.

Richard Mouzon is a psychologist and advocate who is quadriplegic and uses a wheelchair. He has worked on issues involving personal assistance, education, employment and disability rights legislation. He has made several trips to South Africa, working with the South African government's office for disabled persons, and consulting on the development of a national program for inclusion of disabled persons. This project led to several other overseas invitations. For example, Mouzon was asked to go to Bermuda to give a talk on disability rights, and to meet with the government officials there working in disability services.

Many of Mouzon's overseas opportunities came through personal contacts, and a strong interest in achieving inclusion through policymaking. "People here connected me with people in other countries," says Mouzon. He has found that officials and advocates in emerging nations are very often open to networking and using expertise of advisers from abroad. For people seeking similar opportunities, Mouzon suggests researching the political environment and the advocacy activities of a particular country. Many countries have a disability website that provides information about organizations and government agencies involved in disability policy.

You might be a person who is passionate about learning about other cultures and languages, without any particular social interest. Perhaps your passion is anthropology, business administration, history, music or art. Research the options available to do consulting in whatever field you are interested in.

Volunteering Overseas

Service programs are another great way for people with disabilities to get involved in the international arena. These programs offer the opportunity to

There are different ways to go overseas. You could go on an organized program, where many of the logistics are taken care of by staff who know the country well, so you have time to focus on planning for the extra details. You usually have to pay an administrative fee for these additional services, but for some it's worth the extra costs. Another option is to plan your own experience or go on the less expensive programs that may provide less staff assistance. Some prefer the greater independence with this option and learn to rely on the host and expatriate community for information.

spend time interacting closely with people from another culture and being of service to them. Community service and workcamp opportunities come in many forms. Programs may involve physical, social, academic or other types of contributions. They vary in length from a few weeks to more than a year. Examples include building houses with Habitat for Humanity in the United States or elsewhere, distributing food in Bangladesh or participating in an archeological dig in Israel.

Many volunteer abroad experiences involve structured programs or workcamps, such as those offered through Volunteers for Peace. This organization places people in short-term workcamps, where groups of volunteers work on a specific project together. These groups may include people from many different countries. You can also try to arrange an independent volunteer experience by contacting organizations in other countries and asking about volunteering for a period of time while staying with a host family. If you are going to be in another country as part of another type of exchange, such as study abroad, you might also find that you have the opportunity to volunteer while there.

Regardless of the opportunity you choose, you are bound to have a rewarding experience. Angie Allard, a Canadian Crossroads International volunteer who uses a wheelchair, says of her time volunteering at a workcamp program in Malaysia, "My life has been vastly enriched by participating in this overseas service program."

International Conferences

Even if you're not (yet) an internationally known specialist in your field, you can travel abroad and learn more about the issues that interest you by attending international conferences. You're most likely to find out about international conferences if you get connected with national and international groups or associations working in your field of interest. For example, organizations such as The American Archeological Union, TESOL, American Bar Association, International Journalists' Network, Global Fund for Women and other professional associations and nongovernmental organizations hold international and regional gatherings on a regular basis.

Evaluating Overseas Opportunities: Defining Your Interests and Needs

How will you know what kinds of opportunities to seek out? Once you find them, how will you know which ones are right for you? How will you choose?

Some people jump at the first chance they get to go abroad. After all, an opportunity is an opportunity, and they don't knock on your door every day. Jean Lin was attending a youth group at an independent living center in California in 1986 when, one day, the group leader made an announcement about a trip to England. Lin, who has cerebral palsy, was immediately interested in joining the trip. It was the first time she had considered any foreign exchange program, and it seemed perfect. Her parents shared her enthusiasm. Lin enjoyed the program so much that she has traveled with other exchange programs—to Russia in 1991, and to China in 1995. "After my experience, I feel confident traveling," says Lin.

You may, like Lin, have a strong and positive initial gut reaction to a travel opportunity. If you don't, or if you're not inclined to trust your gut reactions, then by all means ask questions. In fact, asking key questions is always a good idea when you are choosing an exchange program. Quiz program personnel about the program mission, policies and procedures, criteria, as well as their ability and willingness to accommodate you. If you're particularly concerned about access and/or support for your disability, discuss this with program staff.

Alona Brown spent a semester in 1996 studying in Alicante, Spain. In searching for an exchange program, Brown wrote letters and made phone calls to several programs that especially appealed to her. She chose a program at Colegio Mayor in Alicante because the director, while on a trip to the United States, actually called her on the phone. "She was so friendly and welcoming, I said to myself, 'This is where I want to go,'" Brown explains. That's when she contacted the Council on International Educational Exchange, the organization that coordinates the program there and has experience in including individuals with disabilities in its programs. "I told them I was a visually impaired student and asked if they could help me," she recalls. "They were willing and happy to help. They answered all my questions."

You may find that some exchange programs lack knowledge or experience related to people with disabilities; but if a particular program appears to suit your other needs, such as academic goals or work experience, don't rule it out without further discussion. Find out whether the program staff are ready to work with you to create an accessible, accommodating situation. Angie Allard was the first wheelchair user ever to apply for a cultural exchange with Canadian Crossroads International (CCI). "Staff and volunteers displayed an impressive degree of openness and willingness to try something new," says Allard. "There were legitimate questions about the very basics like transportation, accessibility and housing. But in the end CCI trusted my judgment about what I could do and what we could do together." Allard was accepted into the program, and given a volunteer assignment in Malaysia.

If, like Allard, you're motivated to be a pioneer in a program that may have less experience, there are resources that can help. The National Clearinghouse on Disability and Exchange can offer a wealth of information and ideas to enable international exchange programs to become more accessible and disability-friendly. See the Appendix for more information on this resource.

Not all sponsoring organizations are so easy to work with. "Be careful when you're checking out programs, and make sure it's a program that's going to be responsive to you," says Susan Brown, whose psychiatric history became an issue during her year as a Peace Corps Volunteer in Ukraine. "If they're not responsive during the interview or initial processes, they may not be that responsive afterwards." Brown was initially denied entry into the Peace Corps, a decision that she successfully appealed. Once overseas, Brown encountered various difficulties and, ultimately, she returned home early. Looking back, Brown feels that if Peace

It's a balancing act between not limiting yourself too much, and focusing in on what you want to do. If you speak French, don't only limit yourself to France but consider West Africa and the Caribbean too. On the other hand, if you want to teach abroad but are open to "anywhere in the world" it will take you longer to narrow it down. Thinking too broadly will make it harder to spread the word about where you want to go and get solid leads and suggestions.

Corps had had a clearer understanding of her accommodations needs before she left, things may have turned out differently.

Other disabled people have reported more positive experiences with investigating and applying for the Peace Corps. Sarah Presley, who has a visual impairment, walked into the national Peace Corps office and requested an application. She received two very different reactions to this request. "One person bubbled over with enthusiasm as she told me what a wonderful time I would have," she recalls. "The other person in the office was less optimistic. He explained many of the challenges I might face, such as the fact that it is sometimes necessary for Peace Corps Volunteers to ride from village to village on a motorcycle. He wondered how I would manage that." Presley was persistent and assertive, and had a successful Peace Corps assignment. "Once I had been accepted, I found the Peace Corps staff in the United States and in Morocco to be very helpful and supportive," she said.

If you're still not sure a particular international exchange program is right for you, ask for names and telephone numbers of former participants who can tell you about their experiences.

Besides the responsiveness of a particular program, several major factors, such as occupational, personal or other interests, will affect your decisions about how and where to spend your time abroad. The following section discusses some of these factors.

The World to Choose From: Where Do You Want to Go and What Do You Want to Do?

Academic Interests

You may choose your destination and activity based on your educational or vocational goals. Working, studying or volunteering overseas can greatly enhance your knowledge of your particular field of study. It can also give you a significant advantage in the job market.

David Dye, who is hearing impaired, was pursuing both scholarly and vocational interests when he decided to study Portuguese in Rio de Janeiro, Brazil. Aiming for a career in international business, Dye knew that Latin America was one of the fastest growing economic areas in the world. He became interested in Mercosur, a free-trade zone made up of some of the most dynamic economies in Latin America at the time, including Argentina, Brazil, Paraguay and Uruguay. Already proficient in Spanish, Dye felt it was important to learn the other major language of the area, Portuguese. "I soon discovered the program at the University of Florida," says Dye. It turned out to be an exciting challenge, leading him to further study with several different exchange programs in other parts of Brazil.

Social or Political Interests

Academic interests may turn into lifelong ideals. Pamela Houston learned about poverty and international development as a sociology major at the University of Oregon, and joined an advocacy group dedicated to education about world hunger. "As I neared graduation, I felt dissatisfied with being involved with these issues on a superficial level," says Houston, who has a mobility impairment caused by cerebral palsy. "I knew the statistics and understood some of the complex causes of poverty, but I needed to touch and see hungry people and do something tangible to make a difference in the world." Houston found such an opportunity with Food for the Hungry International. After a thorough application process, a one-month orientation, a productive discussion about her disability and needed accommodations, and an intense fundraising campaign, Houston spent two years as a volunteer in Peru, where she helped with projects related to hunger and community-building. Perhaps you too will choose your overseas program and destination based on your strong devotion to a particular movement, campaign or philosophy. Like many travelers before you, a compelling need to make a difference in the world might be your prime motivation for undertaking the rigors of going abroad.

Many disabled people have been drawn to international work by a commitment to social change. Cheryl Adams attended a facilitators' training in Todos Santos, Mexico, to learn how to run workshops related to peace. Adams joined sixty other people from 11 countries, all of them committed like she was to "doing what we believe to be the most important work of this decade—learning new ways to resolve conflict." Her interest in this process developed partly from her own experience as a disabled person traveling the world. "I have noticed that using a wheelchair and having a physical challenge brings up other people's fears, guilt and anger," says Adams. She believes that frequently having to operate in unfamiliar territory with unfamiliar people led her to an interest in developing peacemaking skills.

Some travelers go abroad determined to work for equality and human rights for people with disabilities. "My main purpose," says David Oaks, a psychiatric survivor activist, "has always been to meet with other people who are working for self-determination." Oaks is the director of Support Coalition International, an organization that campaigns for human rights and self-determination for people diagnosed with psychiatric disabilities. He has traveled extensively—to Canada, Chile, Denmark, England, Germany and Norway, among others. He has lectured, consulted with psychiatric survivor organizations, helped plan conferences, and supported the development of groups and projects. "I stayed in people's homes, and I met local group members informally," says Oaks. He has arranged these trips primarily by contacting people who subscribed to the Support Coalition's journal.

Commitment to a cause may lead you into extraordinary, even historic situations which will benefit you as much as the issues you are supporting. Mary Lou Breslin went to Bosnia in 1998, about eighteen months after the Dayton Peace Accords were signed, at the invitation of the International Rescue Committee, a development and relief organization that did rehabilitation work with people injured during the war in Bosnia. Breslin was asked to lend support and advice to a coalition of disabled people working for policy reforms. "We worked with an interesting cross-ethnic group of people with disabilities and parents," she says. "We spent a week, about twelve hours a day, developing a statement of principles and press strategy. The Bosnian, Serb and Croat ethnic communities were all represented, all kinds of disabilities, old and young, some recently injured in the war." Breslin adds: "I always feel we got more out of it than they did. It was quite an amazing experience for all of us."

Whatever your ideals and beliefs, you may find them deepened and broadened by acting on them globally.

Disability Considerations

To what degree will your disability influence your decision about where to go and what to do? That may depend on the nature and extent of your disability, and how able you are to adapt to different surroundings.

Many disabled travelers insist that there are really no limits, just opportunities and choices. After all, people with disabilities are living in every country in the world. "You can go almost anywhere in the world and figure out some way to do it, depending on your needs," says veteran traveler Mary Lou Breslin, who uses a wheelchair. "With a good attitude and some help, you can pretty much go anywhere and do anything."

In the overall scheme of things, disability may be a less important factor than you might think, and less important than other considerations. For example, Jean Parker says she's never decided against traveling to a particular place for disability-related reasons. "There would be other reasons, like climate," says Parker. "I don't like cold places."

For some people, living with disabilities might, in fact, nurture an adventurous spirit. Before Marta Lukjan's processing difficulties had been attributed to neuropsychological damage, neither she nor anyone else understood why she had to work so hard at learning, but she was very aware of being different. That awareness was an important influence on Lukjan's decision to study abroad, she says. "My knowledge of being different all the way down to my toes has consciously or unconsciously dictated many of the risks or opportunities I have taken in the past three decades." She knew the usual route wasn't always the right one for her, and was more likely to explore alternatives, such as overseas study.

In considering overseas destinations, do as much research into the local culture and environment as you can to get a sense of factors which may shape your experience there, paying particular attention to anything that you know to be particularly significant in light of your disability. These factors may include physical access, climate, social attitudes and/or customs.

Jean Marchant learned the hard way the importance of local weather patterns in choosing where to go. Marchant was diagnosed with multiple sclerosis, and six years later traveled to Germany. "I didn't have a lot of experience with my disability and the changes that it produces," she recalls. "I checked out the weather in the areas that I was traveling in Germany. The temperature was comparable to Eugene, Oregon, where I was living. But I didn't check the humidity—and that has an adverse effect on my ability to function." She found herself experiencing increased spasticity, partly as a result of the weather. "Think about temperature!" Marchant advises.

While the physical climate aggravates some people's disabilities, the social climate is a bigger factor for other people. When she signed up to volunteer with the Peace Corps, Susan Brown knew she would have limited options in choosing where to go. "You're allowed to turn down an assignment," she says, "but if you turn down too many assignments, they might question whether you really want to do it, since it's a volunteer program." However, she adds, "I was pretty sure they'd send me someplace where I could use my Russian. I was fairly sure I'd go to the former Soviet Union."

Once she received her assignment to Ukraine, Brown began reading up on Ukrainian culture. "I tried to figure out: Are people going to yell at me on the street? What are men going to be like towards women? How unsafe might I feel when I'm in this situation, and how will I deal with it?" She also wrote to other Peace Corps Volunteers to ask about their experiences of, for example, being the only foreigner in a small town. However, these investigations did not fully prepare Brown for what lay ahead. "What I wish I had done," she says, "is to talk with other people with disabilities before I left, to see how they dealt with similar issues." Brown also added that if she had done more research, she probably would have determined that parts of Eurasia might be particularly challenging for her. Brown did experience stress, isolation and depression. She made the decision to accept a medical separation from the Peace Corps, and she still feels that this was the right thing for her to do.

Perhaps as important as choosing your overseas destination, the choice about when to stay and when to leave should be carefully considered. Chances are you will have wonderful, positive experiences, and the problems you encounter will be minor in comparison. But if your international experience turns out to be negative—if your health or safety are jeopardized, or you feel consistently unhappy, especially in a long-term program—then you may be faced with the decision about whether to continue or to return home. "Don't be afraid to quit!" Brown says. "People put so much pressure on each other. But if you need to leave, then you need to leave. Don't feel guilty because you didn't finish this thing you said you'd do. That's just life."

The decision whether to go abroad, and where, is yours. The decision to stay there is also yours—as is the decision to leave early, should it come to that. Wherever you go, whatever you do, you will be the one to make—and live with—those choices. If you want to work, study or volunteer abroad, don't let your initial fears put you off the idea—at least, not until you have explored the possibilities awaiting you. Knowing that your options are open may make it easier to take a leap and try something new.

Most of the travelers who shared their thoughts and experiences for this book would agree with the sentiments of Alicia Contreras, who says, "A lot of people [with disabilities] think, 'I will never be able to travel.' But once you start traveling, it's so good to look at the map and say, 'I've been here! I know someone from here!' It's a great experience."

If you have preconceived notions about where disabled people in general can and cannot go, it's time to banish those myths from your mind! While you certainly need to consider your personal means, health issues and tolerance for difficulty and discomfort, don't rule out any destination because you assume it to be so-called backward, unfriendly to disabled people or inaccessible. People with all kinds of disabilities have gone to all kinds of places, including poorer and rural locations, and have adapted and thrived in those environments.

Jessica Aaron's first trip abroad was to Mexico, for a three-week disability leadership exchange program. "At first, I was hesitant," says Aaron. "I wanted more than anything to travel, as I have studied various foreign languages and am interested in international affairs."

Often it's not until you arrive in a country that you realize many of your worries are unfounded. Obstacles may appear, but you will learn from these situations and have good stories to tell upon return. In the context of a new country, the excitement often balances out the difficulties. Keep this in mind when nervousness or doubts threaten to derail your dreams.

However, Aaron was concerned about being able to be mobile in her wheelchair, and about getting assistance if she needed it. Despite these fears, Aaron did decide to apply for the program, and she was thrilled to be selected. Still, she says, "the excitement I felt was coupled with nervousness; I asked myself how I would get around in an inaccessible place in a chair I couldn't even push by myself. However, as the date approached, I became more and more certain that the experience I would have would outweigh any difficulties I would face." She was right. In Mexico she coped effectively with the physical environment, and found herself doing things she had never imagined doing. "In Nayarit, our first destination, I visited the ocean for the first time in years," she says. "When my chair started sinking in the sand, I got out of my chair and into the warm water to look for seashells." The experience changed her assumptions about what was possible for her. "My trip to Mexico taught me that I can go anywhere I want to, disabled or not," she says, "and that disability is not an excuse for avoiding adventure." Since then, Aaron has pursued adventures all over the world.

While some people have concerns about the physical terrain, others worry about their ability to master a foreign language. Kristin Hoobler has learning disabilities (LD) including dyslexia and was hesitant to travel to a Spanish-speaking country. "Although I have learned how to manage my LD," says Hoobler, "I really struggled with the idea of going overseas and learning a new language. I was told as a young girl that I would be unable to learn another language." However, says Hoobler, "I refused to accept this and I went overseas for a year and learned Spanish fluently."

As Hoobler learned, other people's predictions are not necessarily a good indication of your ability to survive and thrive overseas.

Friends, family members, teachers, exchange staff or physicians, among others, may offer support and encouragement—or they may try to discourage you from taking what they see as a risky trip, given potential problems related to disability or health conditions. For example, Elise Read was elated when she was granted funding for a full year of study in China. Just a week later, however, Read was diagnosed with type I, insulin-dependent diabetes and was suddenly forced to contend with all of the physical and emotional changes such a diagnosis meant. "Originally, my doctors told me that living and studying in China would not be in my best interest," says Read. She held on to her dream, despite their warnings. She delayed her trip for several months, and spent that time adjusting to her new routine of daily injections and blood sugar testing, as well as to the psychological ramifications of coping with a chronic disease. "Fortunately," says Read, "I have a very supportive family and I was persistent enough to convince my medical team to allow me to spend the spring semester studying in China." While there, Read had to contend with such challenges as figuring out how much insulin her body would require after eating a meal that included deep-fried scorpion. "Fortunately, whatever dosage of insulin I'd guessed upon seemed to be correct, as I'm still here to tell the tale," she says.

Here is Ellen Rubin's advice for disabled people who are considering working or volunteering overseas: "You really have to think about what your experiences and strengths are. You have to be confident. If your skills are good, then just say, 'Let me try!' I've had jobs both here and overseas where I've thought, 'I don't know how I'll do it, but I'll do it! I can do it, give me a chance!' Sometimes it works and sometimes it doesn't."

Rubin adds, "If you're a risk-taker, that's really important. Unfortunately, I think so many people with disabilities are not *allowed* to take risks. That really holds us back. You need to have a good sense of what you're willing to try."

Justin Brumelle had already been to Thailand six times before he enrolled in the Council on International Educational Exchange's Khon Kaen program in that country. As a person with a mobility disability, he thought he had a pretty good idea of what to expect and what his comfort zone was. However, he found that one of the program activities that was described as a "90-minute, not-too-rigorous walk through the jungle" was one of the toughest he'd ever been on. "I just wanted it to be over and felt it was pushing my limits a bit too far, yet I wanted to complete it." And with a lot of determination and the support of the other members of his group, he did. "Although leeches and log bridges were not in my comfort level, I realized I could handle them," he recalls. "I pushed my limits and had fun in the process. The program not only showed me my current limits, but it also showed me how much potential exists within me." He recommends that people with disabilities reexamine what they believe to be their physical and mental abilities and constantly revise those beliefs based on new experiences and opportunities.

Are you a risk-taker? If you're not sure, ask yourself some questions: What kinds of risks have you taken in the past? Are you confident in your ability to handle unusual or even unexpected situations? Are you willing to push yourself outside of your comfort zone? Are you able to balance your fears about what might go wrong with strategies for responding to those situations? What skills do you bring to your new international role? What motivates you? What are *you* willing to try? Do you believe the benefits may outweigh the risks?

With so many different overseas programs available, the following are some questions you might ask in evaluating each one. Some of these questions will help you determine whether you will be getting what you expect from the program, while others have more to do with your personal preferences, or with provisions for dealing with the unexpected.

- *How long has the organization been offering its programs? Where is the organization's home base? (Organizations based in the United States are covered by U.S. laws.) How much direct supervision does the organization have over the staff running the program overseas?*

- *What do the program fees cover? Will transportation, insurance or free time activities entail additional costs? Does the organization provide full or partial refund of fees in case of cancellation or early return home?*

- *How are homestays (or host families) selected and what facilities will be available in the typical home?*

- *Do the planned activities (e.g. foreign language classes) fit with the announced objectives (e.g. study)?*

- *What is the exact calendar and daily time schedule of the program, the language of instruction and linguistic requirements? Are participants expected to attend all activities?*

- *What are the qualifications of the instructors, host staff or leaders? How are the exchange leaders selected? Have these people worked effectively with diverse participants, taking into account age, nationality, disability and other characteristics? How accessible and responsive will the exchange leader be to you and other group members and what will be the extent of his or her role?*

- *How are participants selected? Does the application process require letters of recommendation? Is there a deposit required? If so, how large is it and is it refundable?*

- *What arrangements have been made for coping with illnesses, accidents and other circumstances that may require medical services or plans for promptly returning home? Are there any extra charges if a participant has to return before the conclusion of the program?*

Any reputable organization offering an overseas program wants to maintain and build its good name and should be ready to answer questions from prospective participants. Feel comfortable in asking questions until you're satisfied and able to narrow down your choice of programs. You can also ask to talk with alumni or past leaders to help you better evaluate the program and choose an exchange that is right for you.

Summarized from Study and Teaching Opportunities Abroad: Sources of Information about Overseas Study, Teaching, Work and Travel, *1980, U.S. Department of Education.*

Chapter Two

Making Your International
Experience Happen

You have found one or more exciting opportunities to work, study or volunteer overseas. Now comes the work of making it happen— applying to the program of your choice.

In some cases, application and acceptance are fairly straightforward processes. For example, Tanis Doe was an active member of the Canadian Association of the Deaf when the organization was asked to send someone to live and work at the Atlantic College in Wales, staffing the International Deaf Youth Rally. Doe submitted her resume, and was chosen. The Canadian Association of the Deaf raised money for her travel expenses.

The job in Wales was a perfect opportunity with a ready-made funding source for which Doe easily qualified. In contrast, Doe decided a few years later that she wanted to volunteer to work at the school for the Deaf in Brownstown, Jamaica, where she had gotten to know some staff members while on vacation there. "No one sponsored me," she says. "I went on my own. I made my own opportunities." She knew it would be up to her to get the job, and to get herself there. She submitted her resume to the school, along with several letters of recommendation. Once accepted, she applied for a work permit and reached her goal. She worked at the Jamaican school for one year, training teachers and also coaching the children in swimming and general physical education.

The complexity and competitiveness of your application process can vary widely, depending on the nature of the program and how you come to be involved in it. If an opportunity presents itself to an organization or educational institution with which you're already active, and you are already known to have the skills needed for the opportunity at hand, you may be the natural choice. This is most likely in situations involving research and conference delegations, consulting projects, teaching opportunities and exchanges between groups. Your chances of being selected will improve if you have a solid track record in the appropriate field and a longstanding relationship with groups involved in international work.

On the other hand, if you are a newcomer to international work, or approaching a group that doesn't know you well, you may have to prove yourself. Most overseas jobs, and some study abroad programs, are highly competitive and may involve a lengthy application process requiring resumes, references, tests and interviews. For example, Jillian Cutler, who has cerebral palsy, applied for a Marshall Scholarship, a prestigious award for American university graduates to study at a British university for two years. She wanted to study social and political science at Cambridge University. Cutler spent months drafting personal statements and undergoing personal interviews. Her efforts were rewarded when she received word from the British Embassy that she was selected for the program.

For those looking for something less competitive, several exchange programs offer short-term work or volunteer abroad opportunities that don't require a lot of experience or special skills. You might also consider applying for an international internship, which is a good way to gain work-related experience abroad that you can build on for later opportunities.

Most international educational exchange organizations have selection criteria outlined in their application material. Once you have selected the programs you think will best satisfy your interests and desire to study or live abroad, and for which you believe you are qualified, you should contact the sponsors for information and a program application. It is always best to talk with someone— a program coordinator or program officer—who directly coordinates the exchange program. Another option is to contact the overseas study office at your college or university, or an information center at the embassy of the country where you want to go. They will frequently have applications for programs. They can also assist you in determining whether high school or college credit is available for the program in which you are interested, as well as being able to direct you toward other resources.

Telling and Asking: Disclosing and Accommodating Your Disability

Under what circumstances should you tell prospective exchange program staff about the nature and extent of your disability? Some veteran travelers recommend full disclosure, while others sound a note of caution.

"I would not hide the disability," says Don Galloway, who is blind. "I would bring it up up front, so they know what kinds of reasonable accommodations will be needed." As you explore various international exchange opportunities, you should strive for clear communication between yourself and the program staff regarding what accommodation, if any, you may require. It is sometimes the case that the staff will not have much experience accommodating people with disabilities and may not understand what this entails. While you should not be required to answer questions about your disability *during* the application process, it is appropriate for program staff to inquire about disability accommodation *after* they have reviewed your application and accepted you into the program. In order to avoid miscommunications and assumptions, it may be necessary to provide the staff with information specific to your disability and any accommodations required.

Whether public organizations run their own programs overseas or contract out with local partners to run their programs in a foreign country, U.S.-based exchange organizations are covered by the Americans with Disabilities Act (ADA) and cannot discriminate against people with disabilities. International program coordinators must not discriminate against a participant based on a perception of the individual's abilities, and must work to provide appropriate accommodations to ensure that a disabled applicant can participate fully in the program. Similar laws may cover organizations based in other countries. U.S. organizations should make clear to their foreign affiliates and contracting partners the expectation that people with disabilities must be able to participate equally. Organizations in the United States that receive federal funding are also covered by Section 504 of the Rehabilitation Act of 1973. Additionally, some exchange programs, such as those funded by the Bureau of Educational and Cultural Affairs of the United States Department of State, proactively support the inclusion of people with disabilities in their programs. If you encounter barriers with the local program representative, do not be afraid to contact the headquarters office to inquire about their policy on inclusion.

Susan Brown encountered difficulties because of her disability when she applied to become a Peace Corps Volunteer. Because she was seeing a therapist, the Peace Corps put Brown on medical deferment status. With the support of her therapist, Brown appealed the deferment, which involved "a long process of getting letters and writing letters." Her efforts paid off and she ultimately received her assignment to work in Ukraine.

Some applicants have found creative ways to present their disability and their other attributes realistically and positively. Christa Bucks Camacho, who uses a wheelchair, served in the Peace Corps as an urban youth volunteer in Fernando de la Mora, Paraguay. "When I was invited to interview, I prepared by thinking about how the Peace Corps would support my majors in Spanish and international studies," says Bucks Camacho. "I also did a self-assessment of my skills from things I had been involved with earlier. I really emphasized my ability to organize recreational and educational activities for children and teenagers, so my application showed heavily my Spanish ability as well as my abilities to work with children and teenagers." Even though the Peace Corps staff seemed reluctant to ask about her physical condition, Bucks Camacho wanted to put her disability and her coping skills on the table. "One of the things I did was prepare a video I titled *A Day in the Life of Christa Bucks*," she says. "The video helped Peace Corps get to know me in terms of my interests and abilities as well as how I live on a daily basis. I went through my independent living skills, and I also showed them some of the work I was doing as a facilitator on a ropes challenge course. After that, I persistently followed up and that was the key to my success." This strategy proved to have an additional benefit once she arrived in Paraguay. "My personal video was shown to my homestay family so they knew all about me before I came," she says. "My homestay family was wonderful; they welcomed me to be a part of their family."

Your decision about whether to disclose your disability, and how, may also depend upon your personal view of your own disability. Rhonda Neuhaus spent five months in Costa Rica in 1996 with the School for Field Studies. "Part of the process before leaving for Costa Rica involved completing a medical exam form," she recalls. "My doctor filled out the information stating that I wore two BK (below knee) prosthetic legs. Then, a question on another form made me pause for a moment. It asked, 'Do you have any physical limitations?' I pondered this question. If it had read, 'Do you have any physical disabilities?' I would have clearly answered in the affirmative. However, the question did not ask that. The question referred to limitation. I do not see myself as having limitations, and I did not need to request any disability-related accommodations. Until one tries something, one does not know if one can accomplish it. I have had many successes in my life where some people had thought that success would be impossible. So, in answering this question, I wrote, 'No.' Upon arriving in Costa Rica, I saw some initial surprise on part of the staff. However, everyone involved in the program, especially the professors, was open and accepting of me."

Neuhaus felt vindicated in her refusal to equate her disability with the word "limitations." Her study program in Costa Rica, she says, "was an active one, and I fully participated without any problems. We hiked mountains, explored both rural and urban regions and visited protected areas. We studied exotic plant species, performed economic analyses, reviewed watershed management techniques, and analyzed Costa Rica's Organic Law of the Environment. Each day I became more confident, surmounting things that I could have perceived as potential obstacles."

You may want to carefully consider your decision about when and how to disclose your disability, especially if you have a stigmatized disability such as mental illness. Weigh the risks and the benefits, Judi Chamberlin advises. Chamberlin is an advocate for people diagnosed with psychiatric disabilities, and she has traveled the world providing consultation and training services. She advises that if you're concerned about the possibility that an international exchange program may discriminate against you because of your psychiatric history, you may want to withhold this information in the application process—as is your right.

On the other hand, if you have disability-related needs that should be accommodated, then disclosure is the only way to get such accommodations. Talking to the people who will be closest to you, those who will be spending time with you during your exchange, may be the best way to create the safety and stability you need. "People with psychiatric disabilities who think that they might have some sort of stress-related episode or whatever should learn in advance as much as they can about what kinds of support systems they can set up," says Chamberlin. Otherwise, the people around you might overreact to, and mishandle, difficult situations. "If people are not familiar with psychiatric disability," says Chamberlin, "and you say to them, 'I'm just terribly depressed, or I'm having an anxiety attack, or I'm beginning to hear voices,' and people are naive about it, they might send you to a hospital." In some cases, you might be hospitalized against your will, which is something you can avoid with advanced planning and clear communication about your support needs.

When asking for disability-related accommodations, give exchange program staff as much advance notice as possible. This is especially important when requesting equipment that may be hard to obtain, or services that need to be arranged ahead of time, such as sign language interpreting. If the exchange program shows hesitation or confusion in response to your requests, you may want to offer to help in locating appropriate services. You are probably much more familiar with your needs and with how to find appropriate services and resources. Therefore, the more involved you can be in arranging your own support and accommodations, the more likely you are to have a smooth and successful transition to your overseas activity. Information on where to find resources overseas is listed in the Appendix and following chapters.

Fundraising: How to Finance Your Program Participation

If you're independently wealthy, skip this section.

If you're still reading, you may be wondering how you will afford your airfare, lodging, tuition and other expenses associated with overseas travel. Depending on where you're going and what you're doing, your budget can run into the thousands of dollars. That may sound overwhelming, maybe even impossible; but many other people, no richer than you, have garnered the resources to participate in international exchange.

How did they do it? The answers are as varied as the individuals who developed their own fundraising strategies. After Tanis Doe received the opportunity to volunteer at a Deaf school in Jamaica, she collected 40,000 soda and beer bottles on her college campus and returned them for the deposit. "I made $2000," she says. "That was enough for me to go." You will find your own funding sources, and dream up your own schemes for generating the money you need. The same skills and drives that lead you abroad—your talents, your convictions, your resourcefulness, your enthusiasm— can serve as a reservoir upon which you can draw when you take on the task of raising money.

Begin your fundraising process by developing a working budget which shows all the expenses associated with your trip. Some programs will charge a flat fee for everything, including tuition, supplies, travel and housing. Ask the exchange program coordinators if they have a list of costs and/or estimated expenses. In other cases, you'll have to estimate your own expenses—some of which may be unknown at this point, but make your best guess and try not to leave anything out. Go over your budget several times, considering every aspect of your international program, in order to ensure that you have included every expected cost. Think through typical travel expenses, as well as additional costs you may incur related to your disability and access needs. Your budget might include some or all of the following:

- Tuition and program fees

- Airfare

- Lodging

- Ground transportation, such as taxi and/or bus fare, car or van rental

- Meals

- Cost of renting adaptive equipment such as shower chair, portable Braille computer, TTY, oxygen, etc.

- Passport, visa and airport fees

- Travel expenses and wages for a personal assistant, including airfare, lodging, meals, etc.

- Sign language and/or foreign language interpreter

- Travel and medical insurance if not included in program fees

- Materials for your program such as textbooks, guidebooks, etc.

- Spending money abroad for entertainment and cultural events

- Communication, such as international calling cards, Internet access or Internet café fees, telecommunications surcharges, etc.

- Travel gear, such as a passport holder, backpack, first aid kit, etc.

- Gifts for those you meet or live with in the host community and to buy to bring home

Once you have estimated all of these costs, you should be able to come up with a rough total budget for your trip. Next, list any money already committed toward paying for your expenses. For example, your college financial aid package might cover part of your costs. The program may provide scholarships for airfare. Or your family members may have offered to bear some of the costs of your trip. You yourself may have some money saved up that you plan to spend for your travel.

By determining all of your costs, and available resources, you will be able to see how much money you still have to raise. Just as important, you will be able to show potential donors how their contributions will be used. Potential donors will also see how much of your own personal funds you are planning to spend, which gives them an indication of your commitment to your program; and they will be impressed by any support you are receiving from other people and organizations.

Using your working budget, begin to brainstorm about different ways you might generate funding. Consider a multipronged fundraising strategy, especially if you need to raise a large amount of money. That way, if one effort fails to bring in as much money as you hoped, you can move on to other activities that might be more successful.

Don't think you have to do this alone! When it comes to fundraising, two people planning and working are better than one, and five or six are even better! By asking a few friends and acquaintances to join your fundraising committee, you may create just the critical mass of energy you need to come up with great ideas, and to carry them out.

In order to join Up with People on its European musical and service tour, Frank Hernandez had to raise a significant amount of money to pay his participant fees. A talented and enthusiastic young performer who is blind, Hernandez took on this fundraising challenge with confidence, and with a supportive group of friends. He spent a year fundraising, employing a variety of tactics, and he succeeded. The following are some of the projects that helped Hernandez achieve his goal.

One enterprise that proved particularly lucrative, and provided a needed service, was yard sale cleanup. Hernandez assembled a group of his friends, some of whom had trucks, and watched the local papers for yard sale notices. He then sent cards to people planning yard sales, offering to come and clean up their yards afterward, carting away whatever items were still unsold at the end of the day. Exhausted homeowners were happy to call on Hernandez' crew to carry away all their leftover merchandise to help with his fundraising. Once a month, Hernandez and friends organized a yard sale of their own, and sold these items—with the profits going toward Hernandez' program fund.

Hernandez also contacted various clubs, church groups and service organizations, asking for the opportunity to come and make presentations at their meetings. He told his audiences about himself and his background, and about Up with People, a multicultural leadership program for young adults that served communities around the globe through musical performance and community service. He would appeal to these groups to contribute to his tuition fund. He also pledged to return after completing his yearlong tour with Up with People, to do a presentation for the group with stories and pictures.

Finally, Hernandez organized a high-quality musical show at a local theater and charged admission. More on that later.

You may decide to adopt a variety of fundraising strategies, like Frank Hernandez did. Or you may be able to meet your budgetary needs with just one type of activity. Below are some of the most commonly used and effective fundraising techniques used by people planning to work, volunteer or study abroad.

Soliciting Donations from Individuals and Organizations

It may sound simplistic, but one of the most effective ways to raise money for a worthy project is to ask for it! If you can convey the unique importance of your planned overseas program, and its particular value to you and your community, you may find that all kinds of people want to be a part of it. Write letters to friends, family members, acquaintances, business owners, service groups and nonprofit organizations describing your specific goal— whether it be learning a new language and culture, providing leadership at an international conference, or sharing your skills with people in another country. In some cases, you may follow up your letter by meeting with a prospective donor or, as Frank Hernandez did, by speaking to a group of people. Take every opportunity to communicate your dreams and to invite people to support them.

Think about using the media to help publicize your project and to appeal for funds. Study your local radio and television news stations and your hometown newspapers, and identify reporters who regularly write human-interest stories about individuals doing interesting projects. You could be the next story! Send a brief letter to the reporter, describing yourself and your international project. Focus on the aspects of your trip that might appeal to a journalist and his or her audience. For example, if you plan to do a service project, describe the kinds of people you'll be helping. If and when the reporter comes to interview you, provide further information about your project and yourself. Tactfully explain that you are still seeking travel funds, and ask the reporter to mention that in the story.

The success of your appeal for funds will depend on the strength of your message, the value of your planned international activity, your evident ability to accomplish your goals, and the benefits available to your donors. Keep these ingredients in mind when you are asking people for money. Based on previous travelers' fundraising experiences, here are some *Dos* and *Don'ts* to guide your efforts:

Do convey a tone of courtesy and respect. Remember to say "thank you" several times along the way—first for considering your written request, again for meeting with you, again when a donation is pledged, and once more when the check is received. Your gratitude need not be overly effusive, just simple and sincere.

Don't play the pity card. Present your disability in a realistic, straightforward way—as an asset that gives you a unique perspective and, perhaps, a strong commitment to disability issues around the world if that is the focus of your experience. Avoid suggesting, or letting others suggest, that your disability makes you needy or desperate. While such an approach would probably tug some people's heartstrings and purse strings, many others will be turned off—and you won't feel good about it. A more effective tactic, Frank Hernandez says, is to "give someone an opportunity to want to help you, not because you have a disability, but because of what you're doing."

Do focus on the expected outcomes of your international experience, both for you and for your community. Remind your potential donors that you will return home with new knowledge, skills and perspectives that you will share to benefit your community. Talk about what you hope to learn, and how that learning will be useful after your journey is done. Will your time overseas make you a better leader, writer, artist, teacher or citizen of the world? If so, what will that mean to people you work with at home, or to your campus or to local businesses and public officials? Think creatively about outcomes.

Don't talk merely about wanting to do something, without also explaining what you hope to accomplish. For example, while it might be accurate to say "I want to go to Italy," or even "I want to study art in Rome next year," it just isn't enough. A far more effective fundraising statement would be, "I hope to further my artistic and cultural education by studying at a prestigious art school in Rome, with the goal of exploring my own creativity and, eventually, becoming a working artist and a teacher of art." In other words, focus on solid goals and achievements, not just on vague desires. Also include how you will impact others when you return home through mentoring or speaking engagements, for example.

Do provide as much information as possible about yourself and the program in which you are aiming to participate. One idea is to create information packets. Include documents which can help potential donors in considering your request, such as your resume; a description of the exchange program's mission, purpose, history and requirements; fact sheets about your destination country or countries; an overview of the project you'll be working on; perhaps an article you've written on a related topic; and other informative materials. You can send this packet to prospective donors, and to anyone else who requests it and who may have something to offer you.

Don't overlook potential, valuable non-monetary contributions. Sure, cash and checks are nice—but other forms of support can be worth just as much. Perhaps you know a businessperson who travels extensively for her or his job, and gets little time off for vacations; she or he may be willing to draw on accumulated frequent-flier miles to get you a free airline ticket. A medical supply vendor might provide you with enough supplies to last your whole trip. What about a local community newspaper that might like to help you reach your goal, but can't afford to give you money? Instead, ask them to do a feature article about you and your project, with a blurb asking readers to send donations.

Do offer potential contributors something in return for their donation. Think you don't have anything worthwhile to offer? Think again! By working or studying overseas, you may become something of a local expert on the culture, environment or history of the country or region you visit. If nothing else, you will have some great stories to tell! In approaching a group to request funding, offer to share knowledge and stories with your supporters. You can suggest doing this in a variety of ways: regular e-mail dispatches reporting on your activities, presentations at group meetings, articles for organizational newsletters, or photo collages.

Don't make promises you can't keep! Follow through with any agreements. Make good on any offers for future presentations, articles or reports.

Do project confidence in the importance of your project, and in your ability to carry it out.

Don't forget to ask for money! One of the most common fundraising mistakes is to do a great job describing a worthwhile project—and then to neglect to actually ask for a donation! As a general rule, people don't give unless they are asked.

Fun and Funds: Organizing a Fundraising Event

Consider organizing some type of public event involving entertainment, a service or an informational program, and charging admission for it. A successful event can give a real boost to your travel budget. Don't expect your fundraising event to be an effortless windfall, though! It may last only two or three hours, but it can take weeks or months of planning to make everything come off smoothly. With some hard work and creativity, and a little help from your family, friends or colleagues, you can hold an event that will be both profitable and memorable.

When Frank Hernandez was faced with the daunting task of raising thousands of dollars to pay for his participation in the Up with People program, he held a show titled *Songs from the Heart*. The evening featured music on the theme of romance. Hernandez performed, displaying the talent that had convinced the Up with People scouts to invite him to join the group for its tour of Europe. He also recruited several other local performers. He advertised the show and sold tickets in advance. The show was a hit, and Hernandez moved closer to his fundraising goal.

So you're not musically inclined? Think about other events that might appeal to the public, or to a segment of the public. Other overseas travelers have successfully raised money by bringing people together for a single event. Which of the following might work in your community, using your resources and talents?

- A dinner featuring foods of the country to which you are traveling, prepared by you and your friends in a local school or community center with a kitchen

- A slide show featuring photos of one of your previous trips abroad, or photos of your work in your local community

- An evening of readings by local writers and poets

- A wine and cheese party

- A picnic in the park offering refreshments and services such as a car wash

- A mini-film festival featuring videos about the country you're planning to visit

- A dance and ice cream social

- A weekend market with used and donated items for sale

The suggestions above are merely a jumping-off point to get you started brainstorming. You are the one who knows your own talents, connections and interests and what might work best in your community. Use these to plan and carry out an exciting, successful event!

Admission fees are not necessarily the only source of income from an event. You may, for example, hold a silent auction in conjunction with a concert. Ask local businesses to donate merchandise, services or gift certificates. During intermission, have these items on display in the lobby, with bid sheets next to each one. People write down the amount they would be willing to pay for the item, more than the amount written down by the previous bidder. At the end of the evening, the high bidders are announced and the items are purchased.

If your event involves a program booklet, you have another excellent opportunity for fundraising: selling advertisements. When Frank Hernandez organized his evening of musical performance, he asked a local print shop to donate its services to print programs for the show. Then he approached other businesses about placing ads in the program—and with very little effort on his part, he made about $800 from ads alone.

Whatever kind of event you decide to hold, thorough planning is crucial. Don't try to organize something like this all by yourself. If possible, recruit people to help you who are responsible, detail-oriented and committed to your success. Ask each person to take on responsibility for a specific aspect of your event, which may include programming, logistics, publicity or refreshments. Planning an event involves a lot of work; it should not be undertaken lightly. But if you have the time, energy and support, a successful event can bring many benefits besides just the money. People who attend your event will tell other people about you and your project, and this may garner additional support for you. Some attendees may decide they want to contribute more than just the price of an admission ticket, or may invite you to request funds from their organization. At your fundraiser you may meet people who can share valuable information, contacts and guidance with you.

Vocational Rehabilitation

If you're a U.S. college student pursuing a degree program, and a client of your state's Vocational Rehabilitation (VR) Department, you might be able to get VR to cover the costs associated with an international exchange program. Students who receive this funding and plan to study abroad as part of their education should work with their VR counselor to add the study abroad experience to their personal plan. VR funding can sometimes be used to cover particular study abroad expenses. If you have already been approved for funding for tuition, books, fees, a personal care attendant or other assistant, adaptive equipment or a note-taker while studying in the United States, it may be possible to use those funds to cover the same costs while studying abroad.

Tracy Grothe, who has a visual impairment, was pursuing a Master's degree in education with a focus on human services counseling from the University of New Orleans. During this time she spent a semester studying abroad with twenty other students in the Czech Republic and Greece. She received some financial support for her semester abroad from the Nebraska Commission for the Blind and Visually Impaired, which covered her tuition, books and supplies, as well as half of the cost of a portable notetaker with a speech synthesizer, which Grothe used for research, e-mailing professors, collecting data and writing assignments.

In approaching your VR counselor to support an international educational experience, point out that many VR agencies view studying abroad as one way to equalize disabled people's employability relative to people without disabilities. "A job applicant with a disability who has international experience brings that much more to the table to support their qualifications for the job," says Lynnae Ruttledge, Policy and Program Manager at Oregon's VR Services. When an employer learns that a disabled job applicant successfully participated in a study abroad program, or some other international experience, the employer may be more likely to consider the applicant to be highly motivated, creative, versatile and able to solve problems.

You could be eligible for VR funding for an exchange program if you can show a clear link between the benefits of international experience and your vocational objective. Try to make clear that those benefits are not available through participation in a domestic program. Each state has different criteria for deciding what kinds of activities it will fund, but cost alone can never be the only reason to deny funding for participation in a particular program. Jessica Lorenz, a San Francisco State University student who is blind, participated in a Mobility International USA three-week international exchange program to Costa Rica. At the time Lorenz was enrolled in California's VR program, working towards a multi-subject teaching credential with the goal of becoming an adapted physical education teacher. When Lorenz suggested the international exchange program as part of her vocational training, her VR counselor agreed that it would be an added asset to her educational endeavors by increasing her Spanish skills and disability knowledge, both of which would ultimately make her more employable as a teacher.

If your VR department and counselor support your request, it should be written into your vocational plan. If your request is denied, and you genuinely believe the overseas experience is important to your future employability, you can appeal the counselor's decision through the Client Assistance Program. If you present a strong case that participation would enhance your employability, then you may secure VR support after appealing the initial denial. For more information about using VR funding for overseas study or other international exchange programs, contact the National Clearinghouse on Disability and Exchange.

Supplemental Security Income Provision

If a person with a disability from the United States receives Supplemental Security Income (SSI) benefits and has the opportunity to participate in an international exchange program, he or she should apply to have those benefits continue while abroad. There is a little-used SSI provision that allows for the continuation of benefits while participating in an overseas educational program. The *Social Security Handbook* states:

"A student of any age may be eligible for SSI benefits while temporarily outside the U.S. for the purpose of conducting studies that are not available in the U.S., are sponsored by an educational institution in the U.S., and are designed to enhance the student's ability to engage in gainful employment. Such a student must have been eligible to receive an SSI benefit for the month preceding the first full month outside the U.S."

This is an exception to the better known SSI 30-day rule that does not allow for the continuation of SSI benefits while outside the United States for more than 30 days. The requirements to qualify are rigid, but this provision can make it possible for some people with disabilities to gain the international experience needed to enhance future employability.

Another option available to SSI beneficiaries to finance international exchange is an SSI work incentives program called Plan to

Achieve Self-Support, or PASS. An individual with a disability receiving SSI benefits can work with a VR counselor to apply for a PASS, which allows an individual to set aside income and/or resources that will be used to achieve a career goal. Income and resources set aside in a PASS are not included in determining the individual's continued eligibility for SSI benefits. If international experience is approved by the VR counselor as being necessary to advance an individual's career goal, income and resources can be set aside to cover some of the expenses related to participating in the program.

Even if you manage to keep your SSI eligibility while traveling abroad, you should be aware that your Medicaid coverage probably will not transfer overseas. You may need to discuss insurance options with exchange program coordinators and you may ultimately arrange for private medical insurance for the duration of your trip.

Other Government Funding

Some people are able to secure government funding in support of their international exchange objectives. David Oaks traveled to Chile as part of a U.S. delegation to the 1999 World Federation for Mental Health World Congress. Oaks' main purpose during this trip was to work with an international group of people to create a World Network of Users and Survivors of Psychiatry. Oaks obtained partial funding for his travel to Chile from a government scholarship. "I guess I'm lucky," says Oaks, "because I'm working in a network where I find out about certain resources that are available. For instance, government-supported groups in Europe helped pay for my trip when I went to Norway. When I went to England, [a government-supported group] helped me get a bed and breakfast since I did a workshop there."

In order to obtain funding to travel as a leader in the psychiatric survivor movement, Oaks says he had to think creatively. Being an outspoken advocate brought Oaks opportunities and support for his international work, but it also made some resources harder to come by. "Sometimes the system prefers to send people that are not speaking out, rather than people who are working on advocacy or social change," says Oaks. "There may be fewer opportunities for me because of my activism-based approach."

Fellowships and Scholarships

Federal scholarships or awards are also available specifically to support people in studying overseas. Some of these are reserved for graduate students or faculty, while others are available to undergraduates or recent graduates. Some fellowship money will also support unaffiliated scholars, authors, professionals or artists conducting independent projects overseas. For example, Smita Worah, whose field is special education, was awarded a Fulbright Student Fellowship to come to the United States from India and study for a year. The Fulbright Program allows university graduates, graduate students and other advanced-degree students, professionals and educators to study, teach and conduct research abroad in over 140 countries. As a person with a disability, Worah says that it was interesting to see firsthand the impact of U.S. disability laws on accessibility in the United States, and she had new ideas and perspectives on special education when she returned home after completing the program. Another program, the Benjamin Gilman scholarship program, provides grants for U.S. undergraduates to study abroad and specifically targets students with financial need. A third program, the Hubert H. Humphrey Fellowship Program, offers the opportunity for mid-level professionals from designated countries in Africa, Asia, Latin America, the Caribbean, the Middle East and Eurasia to come to the United States for a year of study and professional development. The

Fulbright, Gilman and Humphrey programs are sponsored by the U.S. Department of State and have included people with disabilities.

If you are already receiving financial aid to attend school, you can usually use that same scholarship money for your overseas study program. Your college may also have an alumni association that occasionally supports current students in undertaking special projects. Financial support may also be available for overseas study and research through private foundations and organizations such as the Ford Foundation, the American Association of University Women, the Dewitt Wallace Foundation, the Kellogg Foundation and the Thomas J. Watson Foundation. Civic organizations such as Rotary International or Lions International, certain unions, or special interest groups such as the Sierra Club or Returned Peace Corps Volunteers may be eager to help fund you if your project is compatible with their missions. See the Appendix for further ideas.

Chapter Three

Trip Planning

Your international experience starts long before you leave home, when you start the process of locating resources, assessing living conditions, making arrangements and learning about the host country and culture. Trip planning is key to successful travel abroad, especially for people with disabilities.

Spontaneity has its place, and planning has its limits. Inevitably, you will encounter challenges that you could not have anticipated from the comfort of your own home. When that happens, though, the homework you have done in advance may still save the day.

Similarly, be open to discoveries and opportunities that may await you in your temporary faraway home, about which all your planning might never have given you a clue.

Your Home Away from Home: Arranging Housing

Crucial to your comfort, safety and success during your time abroad will be finding suitable, affordable lodging. While some travelers can simply arrive in a foreign town and find a place to lay their heads, you might have to be more particular. You might have to find a room that is wheelchair-accessible, or you may have other specific disability-related needs such as air conditioning, close proximity to your school or worksite, or extra security. How can you find lodging that meets your requirements, both physical and financial?

It's possible that your exchange program will provide housing in a dormitory, an apartment or in a local family's home. If you're a conference delegate, you may have several hotels from which to choose. In some other situations, you might be responsible for locating and booking lodging for yourself. If that's the case, you may be overwhelmed with the amount of information out there— in travel guidebooks or magazines, and on the Internet. Amid this great quantity of information, you may have to search hard for quality information.

No matter who is making the housing arrangements, you should scrutinize the details carefully. Unless it's explicitly stated, don't assume anything about the level of accessibility. If access is important to you, ask questions until you get satisfactory answers. Even in the United States, non-disabled people often have insufficient knowledge to evaluate access accurately. This problem may be even greater in other countries, where different standards of access apply. Therefore, be specific in asking about particular access features you require, such as doorway widths, bed heights, bathroom configurations and yes, even steps. I once found a Paris hotel room listed as "very accessible" in a travel guide, and this information was confirmed when I called to book a room. When I arrived, I found the front door at the top of three steps. The access touted in the guide referred to the burly bellmen's willingness to hoist wheelchair users up and down these stairs.

Your best sources of information about accessible lodging may be people with disabilities similar to yours—people who understand access needs, and who are or have been in a position to see whether a particular place is truly accessible. Seek out other disabled travelers who have been to the cities and towns you plan to visit, and ask where they stayed and how well it worked for them. Or try to make contact with disabled people who live in those locations, and ask them for referrals to accessible hotels, guesthouses or apartment buildings. If you are participating in an academic exchange, find out if there is a disability service provider at the host university that can direct you to accessible housing.

Your exchange program may be able to work with you to find appropriate housing. Mike Meier, a wheelchair user and a business/economics graduate from Willamette University in Salem, Oregon, participated in a school-sponsored study program in Granada, Spain. He found solid support from his school administrators in resolving issues such as housing. "My study abroad advisor, disabled student services advisor and I formed a team and began investigating accessible accommodations, transportation alternatives and options for classroom sites," says Meier. "My study abroad advisor maintained a positive attitude and a strong commitment to my participation in the program. He expected me to stay positive as well and to provide complete information as to what accommodations I would be needing." In considering the lodging question, this team got in touch with a Spanish organization called Federación Provincial de Minusvalidos de Granada, which had valuable local contacts. "One thing led to another until a family with an accessible home offered to host me," says Meier. "They were excited by the opportunity to host a student with a disability from the United States." This not only resulted in an ideally accessible living situation; it also gave Meier a host family with whom he became very close, spending time together and learning from each other.

When discussing housing with the exchange program staff, describe your accessibility needs as precisely as you can. This will help you avoid ending up in inadequate, inaccessible quarters. It may also help dispel the idea that you require perfect, possibly unattainable levels of access. If at first you encounter negative responses about the program's ability to find accessible lodging for you, encourage program staff to keep trying, and to think creatively about locating and/or creating accessible accommodations. For example, it might be possible to make minor modifications to a dormitory or guesthouse, and thereby meet your access needs. An exchange program that arranges homestay placements might try recruiting a host family with an accessible home by advertising in disability publications, or by contacting a local disability organization. You will find more information about homestay placements in Chapter 4.

If you are an independent traveler, disabled friends and acquaintances may provide you with valuable information about lodging options—or they may provide your housing! Tanis Doe, a wheelchair user who is also Deaf, travels frequently in Latin America, and has also visited several European countries. She says she rarely stays in hotels. "I usually stay with disabled people who have accessible homes," she says. "It's been arranged through the network related to the job or activity I am doing."

It's often a good idea to have other housing options available in case your arranged lodging doesn't work out.

Most disabled travelers agree that planning ahead makes the transition to a different country much easier, especially in finding a place to stay. Leaving your lodging to chance might lead to an adventure—or to unnecessary hassles. "I don't want to spend my whole time there figuring the logistics out," says Jean Parker.

"Some people say that part of the experience is figuring it out. But for me, anyway, when you have a disability, some of that might be true, but some of that's just a pain." For that reason, Parker says, "I will have pretty much established where I'm going to stay, at least for the first little while, until I can figure out what's what."

Parker has enjoyed the opportunities she has found through Servas, an international network of hosts and travelers providing opportunities for personal contact between people of diverse cultures and backgrounds. Through mutually arranged individual visits, hosts and travelers share their lives, interests and concerns about social issues. "You pay a membership fee, and you get a list of hosts, and it gives you the opportunity to stay with a family," she says. "I have had really good success with them."

Another possibility for finding overseas housing is to join a home-exchange network. These resources connect people who are interested in trading living spaces for specific periods of time. The Accessible Home Swap, an online service of the Institute for Independent Living, accepts listings of

To arrange disability-related accommodations, work closely with whoever is arranging lodging and other components of the exchange program you select. Be as specific as possible about any needs or concerns you have in order to ensure that they are understood by the program coordinator.

accessible houses worldwide that are available for exchange. Homeowners describe their neighborhoods, area amenities and the degree of accessibility of their homes. They can also indicate their own travel interests.

Be aware that if you decide to arrange a home exchange, you are personally responsible for the outcome. Most housing exchange networks do not screen or monitor their participants; they merely provide the means for people to connect and make their own arrangements.

Consult the Appendix for contact information for these and other international homestay and home exchange services.

Study the Lay of the Land: Learning about the Country and Culture

Many travelers with and without disabilities find it extremely valuable to learn as much as they can about the country they will be visiting—before they ever leave home. Doing so gives them a sense of what to expect—what resources and opportunities might be available to them as well as possible problems and solutions. These travelers also use advance research to equip themselves with cultural competence: knowledge of the history, customs and beliefs of the particular nation or region.

For Rachael Abbott, who is blind, studying the country has both cultural and practical value. "I research the country, its people and their cultural values—things they hold as important or things that are inappropriate," says Abbott, who has traveled to Chile, Israel and Costa Rica. "I try to research about the places I want to go to, and see if they have accommodations, or what they have available for people who have disabilities."

Researching the country can also open more doors for work, study or other activities. "I do a lot of homework ahead of time," says Jean Parker. "I do a lot of cruising around on the Internet, finding out what's there. Not just in case there's a problem, but also for opportunities. I do stories on lots of things. So I want to know what's there, who's there, what the social and political situations are."

Besides exploring the Internet, Parker seeks out people who can give her firsthand information about whichever country she's headed to. She consults people from other countries who are living in the United States. "For example," Parker says, "one of my housemates is from Tokyo. When I was planning a trip to Japan, I talked with her about transportation in Tokyo. I got good information from her about what was available that I might not have learned from a travel agent." If you don't know anyone from your destination country, Parker suggests going to language schools in your city, and asking for referrals to students from the particular country or region. "Often people in language schools are interested in conversing with native English speakers," Parker explains. "It would be a good exercise to ask them about their country and about what's available there." Foreign students on your local college or university campus may also be valuable sources of information.

Learning some basics of the language can also give insights into the culture, and open doors to international friendships. Frank Hernandez, who is blind, has traveled in Europe, Latin America and Asia, and everywhere he goes he tries to bring along at least a little knowledge of the local language. He writes out the phrases, and then uses tapes to learn proper pronunciation. He also programs some key phrases into his Braille computer, to refer to when he needs them. "It's so nice," says Hernandez, "just to be able to start a conversation by saying 'hello' to someone in their own tongue—especially for someone with a disability, because I think we face more obstacles." Some basic phrases can put people at ease and get strangers talking, he says. "Most people love to teach you about their language and culture."

Planning to Stay Healthy: Taking Care of Yourself

For many people with disabilities and chronic illnesses, maintaining good physical and mental health requires attention to details such as regular medication, proper nutrition and adequate rest. As with other aspects of your journey, planning ahead for health concerns will help you have a more successful international exchange experience.

If you take medications, you will want to do some basic research about your exchange program's policies and about your destination country. Begin by thinking about your medication—those you take regularly, and those you take occasionally when the need arises—and consider how you will get these needs met. Contact your physician and your insurance company for answers to any questions you may have. Your exchange program staff can be helpful in connecting you with facilities and resources in the host country, and in considering additional questions that have come up for exchange participants over past years. Begin researching early in case you need to resolve insurance issues, locate specialists abroad or deal with any unexpected issues.

Here are some suggestions for health-related matters that may require advance research and planning:

Make sure the medication you use is available and allowed in the country where you are going, and that it is available in the same dosage you take at home. If it is not, what are the implications? Are there appropriate substitutes? Make sure you know the generic name, not just the brand name. Find out what steps you may need to take in order to gain approval of its use. Learn what documentation you will need in order to bring your medication through customs. Transport all medications in their original, labeled containers along with documentation of the prescriptions. "I always bring extra meds—far beyond what I would normally need—just so there is no chance of running out," says Tanis Doe, who uses several essential prescription medications.

Find out what immunizations or vaccinations, if any, you will need to obtain a visa into the host country, and whether there will be any problematic interactions between those vaccinations and your current medication or your medical condition. Visit the Centers for Disease Control website or contact the embassy or consulate of your destination country to find out what vaccinations may be required or recommended.

If you need assistance taking your medication, find out from the exchange program staff whether there will be someone on-site who can assist you.

Try to obtain contact information for local doctors near the site where you will be living, including physicians who speak your native language, and those who practice specialties related to your disability or health needs. Also obtain contact information for some pharmacies. Find out what your medications will cost in the host country. Note that some countries require that the prescribing doctor be licensed in that country before a prescription can be filled.

Ask your home physician what medications you can safely take in the event that you become sick with common traveler's sicknesses. If necessary, request that your exchange program provide refrigerated storage facilities for your medications in your living accommodations, at the host site and during short-term excursions.

Health care insurance coverage is another important issue to consider when planning your trip. If you have private health insurance or student health insurance, or if you are covered by a government-funded health plan (such as the National Health Service in the United Kingdom or Medicaid in the United States), contact your insurer to find out whether your coverage will extend overseas. Ask whether your insurance will cover costs for doctor's visits outside your home country and for prescriptions you buy overseas, and whether it places limits on the amount of medication dispensed at one time or the number of doctor's visits or counseling sessions. Find out about specific reimbursement procedures.

Some exchange programs provide health insurance to program participants. If you intend to use this coverage, find out whether there are exclusions of pre-existing conditions or a clause for treatment for unforeseen changes in conditions. Based on the answers to these questions, consider whether you should purchase supplementary insurance. If you decide to do so, shop around carefully. Find out whether the policy will cover your pre-existing disability or health condition, and what limitations might be written into the policy. Some medical insurance plans will also cover travel costs for relatives to be with you in the event of an emergency, emergency evacuation to medical facilities in another country and repatriation of remains in the unlikely event of death.

In addition to resources such as medical care and prescription medications, your health maintenance during overseas travel may also depend upon important lifestyle choices. Veteran international travelers offer the following suggestions:

- Drink a lot of water, especially at higher altitudes, in hotter climates and during rigorous activities such as hiking or working outdoors.

- Drink bottled water to avoid bacterial infections.

- If you have allergies, stay aware of your environment, and try to avoid exposure to known allergens. Also be very cautious about what you eat. If you use an anti-allergy medication, keep it with you at all times.

- Get plenty of rest.

Pamela Houston, who has cerebral palsy and has done volunteer work in two developing countries, offers international travelers with disabilities this advice: "It is extremely important to take good care of yourself, particularly when your body and mind are under stress because otherwise you might become ill." Careful planning and advance research can help you to optimize the conditions you require for staying healthy.

The Right Frame of Mind: Preparing Yourself Emotionally

Especially for first-time travelers, spending time in another country can be a daunting prospect. The decision to go abroad requires careful self-assessment, as discussed in the previous chapter. Once that decision is made, and you're headed overseas, your qualms may fade away amid all the excitement. Or, as some people have found, those qualms may grow larger as your departure date gets closer!

Your chances of having a successful international experience will be greater if you approach your sojourn with confidence and calm. That's not always easy. Anxiety over travel details, thoughts of what can go wrong, and fear of the unknown may all contribute to travel stress. Such worries may particularly, but not exclusively, impact people with psychiatric disabilities. Anyone can feel fear and trepidation when faced with complex travel arrangements, or with the prospect of venturing into wholly unfamiliar territory.

When fears do arise, adapt your coping mechanisms to the demands of travel planning. One university exchange participant focused on her goals and dreams to help keep her anxiety and panic attacks under control. She concentrated on the steps needed to prepare for the international exchange, to avoid worrying about the actual commencement of the program. She also told herself that if she got too anxious, she would just drop out of the program—a back-up plan that she didn't end up using.

If you have emotional or psychological issues that you fear may become exacerbated while away from home, you may want to think through any possible problems, and strategize for dealing with those problems if and when they manifest. Again, your greatest strength is self-knowledge. Use the techniques and skills you have developed to cope with stress in your daily life. You may have a well-developed support system at home; think about how you developed that support system, and plan to create a similar, temporary support system in your foreign destination. Be prepared to explain your concerns and your needs, when necessary, to get the support you need.

If you will be staying with people, they may become your support system. Judi Chamberlin, a psychiatric survivor and a board member of Mental Disability Rights International, offers this advice: "If you deal with these things on a repeated basis, and are afraid it might happen to you when you're abroad, you probably have some kind of self-care plan. And if you're staying with a host family, you should be able to discuss it with them, preferably before you get there." Chamberlin suggests approaching the subject with matter-of-fact honesty, clarity and specificity. Your discussion might begin like this: "Look, sometimes what happens to me is this; and what helps me at these times is this." In short, says Chamberlin, "Set up your support system in advance, even if you're never going to need it." Given the stigma surrounding mental illness in virtually every country, Chamberlin acknowledges that such a discussion may not be easy, and that it may even result in misunderstandings.

Ask your exchange program contact whether you might be able to meet your host family or in-country staff before going abroad via email, letters or telephone, to develop a relationship ahead of time. This might help make transition easier, and aid in establishing expectations.

Planning Support: Arranging Educational or Occupational Accommodations

To carry out the purpose of your trip, you may need to arrange for reasonable accommodations in your classroom or workplace. You will be most successful if you begin this process before you leave home. Educational and occupational accommodations may require obtaining funding, securing cooperative agreements among several agencies, procuring adaptive equipment or rearranging classrooms, offices or schedules.

Chapter 4 will provide more detailed information about different types of disability accommodations that are possible in different school, work and volunteer settings. Arranging these accommodations, however, should be an important part of your pre-planning process, if necessary in your situation.

For example, an educational exchange participant with a learning disability may wish to initiate discussions about necessary accommodations with school officials, disability service providers, his or her rehabilitation counselor and other involved parties. Regardless of your disability, state your needs clearly, and ask very specific questions, including:

- Is the same technology you use at home (e.g. computers with spell checkers) available in the host country? If so, will you be able to access the technology? If not, what alternative accommodations and services can be provided that still fulfill your needs?

- What documentation is needed to get these accommodations or services?

- If necessary, who will pay for your accommodations, tutors or other services?

- Will there be a contact person who is familiar with the provision of accommodations and services to students with disabilities?

- What support systems can you use if you encounter resistance regarding the provision of appropriate accommodations?

- Does the host university or community have professional disability service specialists or are there sources of informal support available to international students?

Your issues and, therefore, your questions will differ according to the nature of your disability. Begin by thinking about the types of accommodations you use at school or at work in your home country. Think of these accommodations as a baseline, but be prepared to think creatively about different accommodations you may use overseas. There are several reasons for thinking outside the box when it comes to arranging your educational or vocational accommodations. First, you may be planning to engage in activities which are not typical for you—activities such as constructing a school, teaching reading and writing in a rural area, exploring cultural facilities such as theaters or museums in an ancient city, studying a foreign language intensively or visiting local community-based organizations to learn about social or political issues. Unusual demands may require additional accommodations. Second, the accommodations you typically use may not be available in your host country, because of limited technological or economic resources, the physical terrain or other differences. Finally, you may discover that accommodations not normally available to you *are* available in your host country. Consider all the possibilities, and choose the accommodations best suited to your disability and to your exchange program activities.

Be flexible when you feel you can—but don't compromise on adaptations or services that you feel are crucial to your successful participation in the exchange program. Debi Duren, a Deaf woman who was a student at the University of Oregon, participated in a workcamp exchange to Costa Rica. Duren's advice for Deaf exchange participants is "to be assertive with their needs for communication, specifically their preferences for interpreters who use ASL [American Sign Language] or other communication modes. And arrange to have some time to get to know interpreters before going abroad." Duren feels this is important in order for the participant and the interpreter to establish a good rapport, and to get to know each other's styles and preferences.

Traveling with a Wheelchair: Manual or Motor?

If a power wheelchair is your usual means of mobility at home, you have an important decision to make when planning to work or study overseas. Will you bring along your heavy, complex, electricity-dependent but beloved power chair? Or will you leave it behind, and instead travel with a lightweight, foldable manual wheelchair? There are pros and cons to both courses of action. Your destination, your personality and your priorities will be the deciding factors.

If you're headed for a modern industrialized nation, such as the United States, you and your trusty power wheelchair may find very accessible conditions—lifts on buses, sidewalks with ramped curbs and relatively easy access to most public buildings.

Many parts of the world, however, still present barriers to those using wheelchairs—and that may influence your decision about what kind of chair will accompany you on your journey. "Given conditions in Russia, most people choose not to take a power wheelchair," says Bruce Curtis at the World Institute on Disability. Curtis is quadriplegic and uses a wheelchair, and has traveled to Russia many times in all types of weather. He recommends that wheelchair users planning to spend time in Eurasia bring along a narrow folding chair. "Push handles are almost a necessity as you will be lifted on many occasions," Curtis adds. "Use tubeless tires or bring along plenty of extra tubes and patch kits. Try to have larger front rollerblade casters installed. This will help prevent the front of your chair from getting hooked up on the cobblestone streets."

People visiting developing countries must consider many factors related to wheelchair maintenance, repair and accessibility. Harriet Johnson has traveled throughout the United States in her power chair, but when preparing to attend a conference in Cuba in 1997, she decided to take a manual chair instead. "I figured if my chair were damaged in transit, as it often is, it might be difficult to get it fixed," Johnson explains. "In 1997, Cuba was dealing with particularly difficult economic conditions and shortages. While their mechanics are legendary for repairing things without standard parts, at that time something like a rubber patch for a flat would have been a big deal." In addition, Johnson had been warned about Havana's limited access and rough sidewalks. "I wanted the flexibility of being carried in a lightweight manual chair," she says.

On the other hand, some travelers prefer the independent mobility provided by power chairs, and they are willing to take on the additional complications and risks these machines involve.

Contact people with disabilities who have lived in or are from the country you plan to travel to. They can be a valuable source of information and advice on available disability-related resources and what to expect when you get there.

Rosangela Berman-Bieler has traveled all around the world, including Latin America, Europe and Asia. Wherever she goes, Berman-Bieler always travels in her power wheelchair, although it cannot be disassembled, folded or easily tossed into a taxicab. Berman-Bieler feels that she wouldn't be herself if she could not move around unassisted. "For years and years I have been totally independent," she says. "It would be a bad experience" to lose that independent mobility.

Riding in a power wheelchair makes it somewhat harder to access various modes of transportation, such as buses, cars and taxis, Berman-Bieler acknowledges. However, she points out that she has an easier time getting around on her own within local areas. With her power chair, she doesn't need someone to push her around. Even inaccessible sidewalks don't create insurmountable obstacles: "I ride in the streets when there are no ramps," says Berman-Bieler.

If you have the luxury of shopping around, you may find a wheelchair that gives you the best of both worlds. Mary Lou Breslin did. "Everyone told me I couldn't bring a motorized wheelchair to Russia," says Breslin. She resisted this well-meaning advice. "I really felt like I couldn't work without it, that I wouldn't be effective if I were pushed around," she says. It so happened that she was in the market for a new chair anyway and, based partly on travel considerations, she purchased a lightweight power chair, which had a detachable frame. "It was fabulous," Breslin says. "It's small, compact, very sturdy." Best of all, the chair could be taken apart when necessary. "You can take the chair off the drive train, and take the foot pedals off, the armrests off, fold the back down, and put the seat on the back seat of a cab, for example. Two plugs, two turn bolts, and a couple other things need to be undone to take it apart." She adds, "It wasn't easy, it's not the kind of thing you want to do every day"—but the chair offered both portability and independent mobility, which greatly enhanced Breslin's overseas experience.

Breslin advises careful consideration of the manual-chair-or-motorized-chair question. "If you can function, you should go with a push chair in most places," she says, "because it does make the lifting a lot easier where there's one or two steps to navigate. But I prefer independent mobility. I think people should go with what they're comfortable with, and what they really need."

Charging wheelchair batteries was once something of a hit-or-miss proposition. Recently, however, travelers are reporting few if any problems. "Everyone told me there would be problems charging the chair in Russia because of the voltage issues, but there just weren't," Breslin says. Nor did she have trouble in Bosnia or Japan. She simply brought along voltage converters, which can be purchased in any luggage store or electronics retailer. Of course, this will not work if you are traveling to remote rural areas with unreliable or nonexistent electricity.

A similar decision may face you if you have a mobility impairment but typically do *not* use a wheelchair at home. If you expect to be traveling long distances regularly, such as touring cities, going from village to village or traversing the grounds of a workcamp, or if your balance is an issue, consider the possible benefits of renting or bringing along a lightweight wheelchair; ask wheelchair users for tips and practice using a wheelchair on different surfaces and terrain before you leave.

Traveling with an Assistant, Sign Language Interpreter or Similar Support Person

If you need assistance with personal care, communication, reading, navigation or other tasks, one of the most critical parts of your travel planning will be making arrangements for obtaining the help you need. This, too, involves some decisions. You'll need to decide whether to bring along a full-time helper, get assistance from another member of your travel group or find an assistant in the country you're visiting.

These choices will depend upon a number of factors, including the length of your trip abroad, the type and amount of assistance you need, the availability of such assistance in your destination country, the willingness of your traveling companions, and your financial situation.

Depending upon these factors, there are several different scenarios you can consider. You may negotiate with a fellow participant to provide your assistance in exchange for some travel expenses. In a study abroad program, your sponsoring school might compensate a fellow student with work-study wages or scholarship aid for assisting you. If you make such an agreement, make sure that both of you are comfortable with it, and that the participant assisting you understands and accepts his/her responsibilities.

If you use personal assistance, such an arrangement offers advantages and disadvantages, in comparison to traveling with a full-time attendant. Jenny Kern, a quadriplegic, has chosen during some of her trips overseas to get the attendant care she needed from a co-worker. This was not an ideal situation, she concedes; it involved "minimizing what I needed." However, she made this decision partly in order to save money for the program she was working for, and partly because "I'm not crazy about having help," she says. "I tend to be a risk-taker. I like doing it for myself."

If you have solid contacts with a well-resourced organization in your destination country, and if you do careful advance planning, you may be able to obtain the assistance you need after you arrive. For instance, Dr. Abdul Salam, who is blind, traveled from the United States to Uganda to work as a volunteer adviser to a non-governmental organization concerned with small-scale agriculture and economic development. The organization that sponsored the exchange, ACDI/VOCA, arranged for a local university student to assist Dr. Salam with mobility, reading and notetaking.

You may also be able to make arrangements yourself. You might request information on available assistance services from disability organizations in your host country. One advantage of this is you can save on travel expenses by finding people locally, split the work between people so as not to overwork one person, and replace an assistant more easily if the situation isn't working out. Also, it can give you access into the language and culture of the host community.

Alona Brown, who is also blind, spent a semester studying in Alicante, Spain. In this new environment, she knew she would need mobility training. To succeed at her schoolwork, she would also need readers and tutors. She made sure to communicate her access needs to the program director and to the resident program director, who in turn used ONCE, a Spanish disability organization, as an information resource. Forming a relationship with a local disability group was essential to making Brown's study abroad program a success. By the time she arrived in Spain, everything she needed had been arranged. Her mobility training, provided through a contract with ONCE, went well.

If you get services overseas, ask questions and get assurances before you leave home. Do not assume that someone else will make the arrangements for you!

If you need frequent or extensive support, or if this service cannot be found within your travel group or your host organization, you may decide to hire your own support person from home. For instance, if you will need a sign language interpreter, it's not likely that you will find someone within your group who can provide this service. Additionally, it is difficult to find sign language interpreters who are able to interpret sign languages other than those used in their own countries. Deaf exchange participants have dealt with this in a variety of ways. Some participants have used interpreters from home who were willing to work for a flat daily rate rather than an hourly wage. Others have used advanced interpreting students who charged less because they were not yet certified and they were very interested in traveling. The Deaf participants involved in these exchanges agreed to use these interpreting students after meeting with them and determining that the situation would provide adequate interpretation for the program. If you can guarantee a certain amount of free time to your interpreter while abroad or the person is motivated by the idea of travel, you will be in a better position to negotiate. Some Deaf participants on long-term exchanges have found that after being abroad for a while they were able to transfer to using the sign language of the host country, and didn't need interpreters as often. If you connect with members of the Deaf community in the host country, you'll have greater opportunities to practice the local sign language and may need your interpreter's services less frequently.

Sarah Beauchamp traveled to Scotland on a university exchange program. She brought an American Sign Language (ASL) inter-preter with her from home, but also had the opportunity to connect with the Deaf community in Scotland and learn British Sign Language (BSL). "Besides eating haggis (which is an entirely different story)," Beauchamp says, "my experience in Scotland also provided me with the most amazing cultural experience: learning BSL. It was completely different from ASL. Learning and signing BSL made me feel more like I was in a foreign country, compared to the familiarity I felt when speaking English." Beauchamp continued to use the ASL interpreter from home when needed, but found ample opportunity to practice her new BSL skills. "I even ran into people at pubs who knew BSL!" she says. "I was so excited and felt very liberated that I could communicate and have a good time simultaneously."

If you hire someone from your home country to provide any kind of support, this entails several important steps: recruiting the right person, agreeing upon duties and terms, securing additional funding and obtaining necessary documentation (such as passports and visas).

Mary Lou Breslin describes the perfect travel helper this way: "A good attendant with the right physical skills and also the right attitude, because you run into all kinds of stuff. You have to go with the flow and you absolutely have to maintain your cool"— and so does your assistant. Consider also the more rigorous conditions you and your helper will encounter in other countries, and find someone "who is very competent in handling situations that come up where there's a lot of unusual kinds of lifting. When there's not an aisle chair in an airplane, for example, which is very typical in Eastern Europe, or where the bathrooms aren't great."

Compatibility is important too. If you're a highly adventurous traveler, you probably don't want to bring along someone who's timid or overly cautious. If you like to stay up late or, conversely, you function best in the early morning hours, your travel and personal care routines will run more smoothly if your attendant shares your preferences.

Jenny Kern, who has traveled to China, Kenya, Uganda, Mexico, Uzbekistan and Pakistan, looks for an attendant who can share the good times and the bad times. "It's become more important to me to feel like I have built-in support," says Kern. "As I'm more in tune with my emotional life, I need to know that I'm going to be able to share that. If I need to have a good cry, I need to be sure this person isn't going to be freaked out by it." She recalls a particularly difficult trip, her first overseas experience, for the Forum on Women in China. Dealing with access barriers, obstinate officials and physical discomforts, Kern felt a lot of anxiety. In contrast, her attendant remained cheerful throughout their time in Beijing. "On one hand, it was helpful," says Kern. "In another way, I felt my fears were invalidated." Depending on the challenges you foresee on your particular journey, the ideal travel attendant may need to be ready to play a more proactive role than would be the case at home. "That person may be your conduit to communicate with somebody who's in charge, in an inaccessible place," says Mary Lou Breslin. In that event, assertiveness and good communication skills would be important qualities for your assistant to possess.

How can you find a good travel assistant? "The best thing to do is to ask around," says Breslin. Pass the word among "friends, colleagues, students in your community who have traveled," she advises. Another approach is to place ads in newspapers, or post notices in community centers, colleges and other public places. Breslin also advises that you list the specific qualifications you are looking for. "I prefer someone who has traveled before, who's had experience with airports, airport security, wheelchair dismantling and aisle chairs," she explains. "But it's not a requirement."

Remember that if you plan to bring a person from home who will provide services for you, you must double your attention to certain aspects of your travel preparations. As discussed above, an assistant can increase your expenses, as you must usually pay some or all of his or her expenses, including airfare, lodging, ground transportation and food. Be sure to build this into your travel budget, and fundraise accordingly. It is important to be clear about what the payment arrangements will be—wages, a stipend or expenses only? Does it include transportation, food, lodging, etc? Be sure to budget for such items, if payment will include them.

Make sure the person providing services to you has a passport and other required travel documents. If you're traveling to a country that requires a visa, investigate thoroughly to determine what documentation is required. While your participation in an exchange program, conference or job will likely support your visa application, your assistant's application will need to be written differently, to describe her or his role and responsibilities.

Disability organizations in the host country can often provide information on accessibility and disability-related resources, and important cultural information about perceptions of disabilities in that country.

Be sure to research any additional issues related to international travel restrictions for an assistant. Harriet Johnson discovered one key issue involved in traveling to Cuba: The U.S. government requires a State Department permit to travel to Cuba, due to the embargo against that country. This policy had prevented Johnson from going to Cuba once before in the 1980s. "I had considered going to Cuba with a delegation of lawyers," she explains, "but the permit obtained for the group did not cover personal assistants. I inquired about getting the permit modified, but the sponsoring organization wanted to keep a low profile with the U.S. government, and given the political situation at that time, I didn't blame them." In 1997, with this concern addressed, Johnson was able to travel to Cuba because the State Department permit covered both conference participants and attendants.

Traveling successfully with an assistant, interpreter or other support person requires more than just budgeting and taking care of visa requirements. The close proximity of travel, hectic schedules and the stress of dealing with obstacles and strangers' attitudes can create fatigue and tension, which can sometimes disrupt your working relationship with your travel assistant. Both you and your helper may become irritable, even uncooperative. Richard Mouzon, a quadriplegic who has traveled extensively with a personal attendant, advises: "You have to have patience. That's what wears on me towards the end of a lot of trips."

You can avoid trouble with your assistant by planning ahead, and by communicating clearly. Susan Brown, who has accompanied and assisted several different disabled travelers, feels it's essential to make expectations clear, including:

- The duties, hours and rules involved in the job

- A complete travel itinerary

- Any information you find in your research about cultural norms, climate, etc.

- The kinds of activities you and your assistant will be involved in

- Suggestions for how to dress, based both on cultural norms and the types of meetings or other activities your assistant will be attending

In addition, Brown urges disabled travelers and their support people to discuss possible scenarios involving prejudice and discrimination, and to talk about how to deal with those situations when they arise. "Watching people do discriminatory things is frustrating and overwhelming," she says. "It made me angry many times. Be prepared for that." Brown adds that you're probably going to get stared at, people may say things and you may get ignored. The person at the desk may ask, "What does she want?" Brown advises: "You're going to have to deal with that. I would tell the person who's doing the hiring that you need to be really clear about what you want in those situations. Do you want the attendant to ignore the person who's asking an offensive question? Or will you or your attendant prepare a rude reply? Or will you advise your attendant to be very polite, smile and answer for you?"

To avoid burnout on longer trips, Brown recommends arranging for a backup for your primary support person, if possible. This might be a friend or acquaintance in the destination country, a fellow traveler or a worker hired from a local agency—"just someone to do a little bit of work, like to help someone go to bed one night, so the assistant can crash really early. If there's any way that can happen, I think that is invaluable." If that is not feasible, try occasionally to allow your assistant even a short time off during the day—perhaps by "making sure that you are set for the next hour or two while you read your book or whatever, and the attendant can just go away." Brown adds, "If there's any way you can swing it, letting the attendant have their own room, at least sometimes, makes a huge difference."

Finally, show appreciation for efforts of the person providing services to you. "People have been really nice to me," says Brown, describing small but meaningful rewards offered by travelers for whom she has worked. "Like, they know I like chocolate, so they buy me chocolate every once in a while." To Brown, these little gifts are a way of saying, "Thanks for being here!"

Animal Companions: The Pros and Cons of Traveling with Service Dogs

Some disabled people rely upon dogs for various kinds of assistance including mobility, reaching and safety alerts. If you use a dog, you will need to decide whether to bring him or her with you during your international exchange.

On the plus side, having a dog with you may allow you to maintain the independence abroad that you have come to expect at home.

On the other hand, depending upon where you are going, there are serious drawbacks to bringing along a dog. Some countries have strict quarantine laws, which make it virtually impossible to come into the country with a dog or any other animal. Don Galloway encountered this barrier when he began his job as Peace Corps director in Jamaica. Due to the country's quarantine laws, Galloway was not allowed to bring his guide dog with him.

Even in the absence of such quarantine laws, Galloway never travels abroad with a guide dog now. Culturally, these animals would be a problem "almost everywhere, except parts of Western Europe," says Galloway. "In some cases, a dog is looked upon as being a very unclean animal," he points out. The breeds most often trained to be dog guides may be the most problematic in some countries, Galloway adds. "Colonial powers used to use dogs for crowd control," he says. "They used German shepherds and Belgian shepherds, so people are very frightened of those dogs."

Like Galloway, Jean Parker thinks it best to travel without a dog in tow. When she did have a guide dog, she left him at home when she traveled abroad, choosing not to spend her time and energy negotiating various laws and customs regarding dogs. In addition, she worried for the safety of her dog in some environments. There are places where people are cruel to animals. Parker says, "I don't think it's fair to knowingly put your dog in danger."

However, with enough careful planning, and in the right environment, a dog guide can be an asset. Denise

Be prepared to approach your accommodation needs creatively, and be flexible about trying new disability-related supports and services.

Decker spent a three-year fellowship in Brazil with Partners of the Americas. She designed and conducted a project called Encouraging Independence that trained volunteers to help people with disabilities in Brasilia, the project site. Decker did bring along her dog guide, named Quadrant, who played a very important role in her trainings. "Bringing a dog guide to Brazil," Decker says, "offered an interesting set of potential difficulties, which I overcame by making advance arrangements and working with my Brazilian counterparts. I had to arrange permissions with the airline and the organizations where we would research and train. People are generally willing to grant these permissions, but they can take time, especially when individuals may not be accustomed to working with animals, even trained ones." She adds: "I found it useful to plan how to describe what Quadrant does for me and to have the name of a veterinarian in case of need." Her dog was featured in a newspaper article due to its uniqueness in Brasilia.

You should also contact your overseas school or host organization to discuss accommodations necessary for your service dog. Marisa Saldaña, who is blind and travels with a guide dog named Acer, went to Victoria, Australia to study at La Trobe University. Before applying to attend La Trobe, Saldaña contacted the college where she would be living, as well as a staff member in the International Programs Office at La Trobe, and an instructor from the Guide Dog Association in Victoria. "Conveniently, the college offered me a room on the first floor of the dormitory and close to a relieving spot for Acer," says Saldaña. She had a very positive experience, both with her exchange program and with her service dog.

If you are considering traveling internationally with a dog, contact blind organizations and/or guide or service dog schools in your destination country to find out how practical that would be. Also contact the country's embassy or consulate to find out about documentation required for bringing a dog into the country. Many countries require up-to-date vaccinations and sometimes microchipping (an identifying computer chip placed just under the skin of the animal). "You need to be really sure you know what the laws are and cultural norms are," says Jean Parker. In some countries, she adds, people are beginning to use guide dogs more frequently. Arm yourself with information, and make the best choice for you—and for your dog.

Group Orientation: Becoming Part of the Team

If you will be traveling as part of a delegation, school group or other exchange involving a group of people, you may find that you have a built-in support system, and a valuable resource for access and accommodations. This resource will prove most effective if you and your fellow travelers spend some time on team building. However, do not take for granted that this informal support system will offer consistent support; expectations need to be discussed and realistically planned for.

The key to team building is good communication. Recognize the importance of sharing information about what you need from the group, and what you can offer to the group.

Jean Parker joined a delegation, sponsored by the Center for Global Education at Augsburg College, to travel to Central America, including Honduras, El Salvador, Nicaragua and Guatemala. As a blind traveler, Parker needed to make sure she could count on occasional mobility assistance, and that she had access to all relevant information. "When the group first got together, I asked for some time on the agenda at the introductory meeting," says Parker. "I explained how the cane works, that when the cane hits something, it's okay; how to walk as a sighted guide; just the basics like that."

Another time, Parker visited several towns along the U.S.-Mexico border with a delegation sponsored by Border Links. This trip involved both learning and service. Delegates studied issues such as immigration, trade and globalization, and they also helped with painting and other chores in some churches. Again, Parker spoke honestly about her participation in the group's activities. "I told them, ahead of time, my expectation was that I would be given a task along with everybody else," she says. In both cases, Parker found that her explanations were well received and helpful to everyone. "By and large, people who go on exchanges are open to new things," Parker says. She advises disabled travelers to invest the time and energy necessary to educate and build good working relationships with other delegates. "The more preparation you can do, the more setting out what your expectations are, and finding out what their expectations are," she says, the greater the chance that "you can avoid trouble, awkwardness, and wasting time."

In preparing for a 1995 Mobility International USA trip to Russia, the group of people with and without disabilities bonded quickly and worked together well. According to Mary Ann Higgins, exchange coordinator, a critical part of the pre-trip orientation was talking about how they were going to work together as a team so that everybody could participate equally. Higgins explained that curbs, stairs and less than accessible transportation were simply the reality that they would face daily in Russia, but that in working together as a group, those barriers would become unimportant. In their group discussion, people who used wheelchairs talked about how they preferred to be lifted and pushed, people who were blind talked about how they liked to be assisted, and people who were Deaf discussed what they needed to get the most out of the experience. Everyone also shared what he or she had to offer the group. It made for a much more successful and fulfilling experience for everyone.

Remember that in dealing with a group, accommodation is a two-way street. Just as you may expect other people in your group to make adjustments or even compromises in order to include you, likewise you should expect to make adjustments, share responsibilities and consider other people's needs in addition to your own. "When traveling in a group, you must always keep in mind that your needs and wants are not the only ones, and each group member will have to make sacrifices," says Emily Johnson, a paraplegic who participated in the Semester at Sea program, a study program which included visits to South America, Africa and Asia. To illustrate her point, Johnson describes a trip she and her fellow students took from Mombasa to Nairobi, Kenya, on an old, inaccessible train. Despite the problems this mode of transportation posed for Johnson, it was much preferable for all the other students because it was inexpensive and fit their limited onshore schedule. "Although a plane flight would have been more accessible,"

If you are traveling as part of a group, be proactive in addressing expectations and support issues to avoid assumptions on both sides. Be clear about any support you would like from the group, but also make sure they know what things you don't want them to help with, so they don't jump to conclusions about your needs.

Johnson says, "it was in the group's best interest to take the train. Therefore, I chose to make the train work." This was not easy. "The hallways were about the width of shoulders—way too narrow for my chair to fit," Johnson recalls. "After my friends got me and my broken-down chair through the door of the train, I had to be carried down the hall to our coach. Because it was so narrow, it took two of the guys with us to carry me—one behind me holding under my arms and the other in front holding my knees. It was quite difficult, mostly because we could not stop laughing!" Johnson's willingness to join her friends on a less-than-accessible train ride was rewarded with solidarity and support from them in working around the barriers.

Packing: Making Sure You Have What You Need

Your final step in preparing for your trip abroad will be packing. This should be a carefully thought out process. Keep in mind both day-to-day necessities and what you'll need if things don't go as planned. When Elise Read, who has diabetes, went to China for a study abroad program, she "set off for Beijing with an extra suitcase packed specifically with double the supply of medications I would need for my four months abroad (just to be safe)." These extra supplies gave her a sense of preparedness and peace of mind in embarking on this journey.

First, pack a small bag with items that are absolutely essential, to carry with you in transit. Rosangela Berman-Bieler, in her travels around the world, has lost her luggage more times than she cares to remember. "Carry one change of clothes, as well as necessary [medical] items or supplies, in your carry-on bag," Berman-Bieler advises. In addition to the necessities and accessories that any traveler would pack, be sure to think about any items you may need related to your disability and/or to your travel plans. When packing your luggage, consider both what you expect to be doing overseas, and possible situations that may arise unexpectedly. "Bring everything vital," says Jenny Kern, who has traveled to Uzbekistan, Uganda, Costa Rica and several other countries. For example, says Kern, "It makes sense to bring clean syringes to Eurasia or Africa, anywhere there would be concern about contaminated needles. If you have an emergency and you have to go to a hospital, you have your own needles. It's realistic to be concerned about HIV."

Based on the stories and tips shared by people who gave input into this book, the following is a list designed to help you begin thinking about the kinds of things that you may need to bring along when traveling internationally.

- Replacement parts for your wheelchair or other adaptive equipment

- A toolkit for maintaining and repairing your wheelchair or other adaptive equipment

- Batteries for hearing aids and other equipment

- A portable commode chair, if you may be staying in a place with an inaccessible toilet

- Catheter supplies

- Paper or fabric masks to filter out dust and germs

- Doctor's letter, translated in generic terms in the language of the country

- An ample supply of all your regular medications, including extras in case you lose some, or in case you need to take higher dosages due to unusual conditions

- Emergency medications, in case you need them

- Written prescriptions for all your medications

- A list of the generic names of all your medications (physicians in other countries may not always recognize the brand names)

- Clean syringes

- Voltage adapters and extension cords for your electrical equipment such as battery chargers, ventilators and nebulizers

- Sign language/foreign language dictionaries

- Extra pants readily available in case of accidents

Your Best Resource: Developing Disability Community Contacts

One of the best things you can do, as you plan for your trip overseas, is to reach out to people with disabilities in the country or countries you will be exploring. Most of the experienced travelers who offered comments for this book emphasized how important such contacts can be, for helping you plan and deal with the problems that arise when your best-laid plans go awry and for increasing your perspective on the host country. "You should always try to connect with an indigenous person in that society with a similar disability," says Don Galloway. Provided they are knowledgeable, "they can show you the ropes," says Galloway.

Disability organizations abroad may be able to assist with accommodation arrangements; providing referral to local disability-related resources; locating personal assistants, sign interpreters and mobility guides; and advising program participants on accessibility in the host country. They may also be a good resource for finding accessible housing as their members may already have accessible housing and be interested in hosting a person with a disability from another country.

Rosangela Berman-Beiler travels abroad frequently in her role as an adviser to the Inter-American Development Bank. Wherever she goes, she finds that the most reliable and informative travel planning resource is the host country's disability community. Whether she's looking for wheelchair-accessible ground transportation, suitable lodging or information about the area she's planning to visit, Berman-Beiler first reaches out to her fellow wheelchair users and other people with disabilities. "I always try to find a local disabled person to help me," she says. If she doesn't already have these contacts in an area to which she is traveling, she locates them in a variety of ways: she searches the Internet, calls international organizations with affiliates in the country and inquires at local independent living centers, rehabilitation centers or even hospitals. "I keep a folder in my computer called 'Travel'," says Berman-Beiler, "and everything I collect I keep in there—who I talked to, what they helped me with, what services were available—for future reference."

These disability community contacts have enriched Berman-Beiler's travel experiences, as well as helping her out of some difficult situations. Once, on her way to Mexico, Berman-Beiler's wheelchair was damaged, leaving her without independent mobility. Airline officials had told her that nobody in Mexico sold or repaired power chairs. She refused to believe that, and so she spent a full day in her hotel room, phoning Mexicans with disabilities that she knew. Eventually she was referred to a wheelchair repair shop owner who was also paraplegic. He had a van with a lift and responded to Berman-Bieler's pleas for assistance. That evening, he picked her up at her hotel and drove her to his workshop, where he had another wheelchair from which he took parts. He kept his staff working on her wheelchair until 11 pm, and succeeded in fixing it. "It was a totally difficult situation for me, and he saved me without even knowing whether the airline would pay him or not," says Berman-Bieler. He also became a close friend. "That evening we went to have dinner in Mexico City," she says, "and he showed me the old part of the city and its ruins."

Disability contacts abroad, both individuals and organizations, can be an important resource for travelers with all kinds of disabilities. People with psychiatric disabilities may find needed peer support in adjusting to new environments and stresses. Exchange participants with learning disabilities may find people who can help them locate tutors and/or strategize for other types of learning supports. Deaf travelers often find Deaf community contacts that offer valuable information about the local Deaf culture, finding interpreters and learning the country's sign language. Travelers with chronic health conditions may connect with local people with similar medical needs who can refer them to specialists, help find medications and supplies, and make suggestions for appropriate foods that are available locally. Traveling would be more difficult, says Berman-Bieler, if not for the alliances that we have among disabled people.

By considering your needs creatively, researching your exchange program and your destination country thoroughly, planning ahead carefully and developing disability contacts, you will increase your chances of having a successful, productive and satisfying international experience. You may find that this planning process becomes a journey in itself!

Chapter Four

Adjustment to Living in Another Country

You've made it! Your searching, decision-making and planning have paid off, and you are actually traveling to a distant country, excited and ready for your international experience.

This is just the beginning. A whole new set of opportunities and challenges will greet you on the other side of that international border. Getting there, settling in and adjusting to a new environment and lifestyle will require careful strategizing on your part. How can you make your trip overseas smooth and safe? What can you expect once you arrive? What accommodations and adaptations might be available to you? What will be your role now as a foreigner in a different culture?

Many veteran travelers with disabilities advise going abroad fully prepared, but also open to new ways of doing things and unexpected twists. "You can't always plan," says Jean Lin, who has cerebral palsy and has traveled to Russia, China and other countries. "So you have to adapt." Embrace the unknown—foreign cultures and conditions—and everything you bring to your travel experience, including your disability. Be flexible, resourceful and, above all, positive.

"Work with your situation, not against it," advises Emily Johnson, a student with paraplegia who participated in a Semester at Sea program. "I found that my wheelchair enhanced not just my experiences abroad, but also those of the people I traveled with and of the local people I met along the way."

Being an effective international student, volunteer or worker depends largely upon the attitude you take with you. Heather Harker, who is Deaf and has traveled widely, admits that she had approached her earliest overseas experiences with trepidation, fearing she would confront insurmountable obstacles. She learned from experience that she was far more capable than she realized. "It was actually my own perceptions that had created the obstacles. Once my own heart and mind underwent a paradigm shift and perceived the obstacles as opportunities to challenge myself, I could use my passion and confidence to make a difference." That conviction has guided Harker's approach to all of her subsequent trips abroad, and her growth as a person.

Armed with solid information, a positive attitude and a creative, practical imagination, you can tackle your arrival and your adjustment process with confidence. As you arrive and settle in, you may need to negotiate obstacles; if so, you will find or develop the resources you need for access and accommodation. This process may turn out to be the very heart of your journey—to make yourself at home in a faraway place, and to create conditions which will enable you to do your best work.

Getting There

The logistics of overseas travel can be a challenge, even for the most intrepid traveler with a disability. Experience is an effective teacher, and seasoned sojourners have learned strategies for handling flights, customs procedures and other aspects of entering a foreign country.

Airports and airplanes can sometimes present access problems for international travelers with disabilities. If you travel with a power wheelchair, you risk damage each time you check in, as your precious chair becomes just another piece of luggage. To decrease this risk, prepare your chair for travel, and stay involved with the process right up until the time you board the plane. Some tips from frequent fliers who use wheelchairs include:

- Provide clear instructions—both orally and in writing—for how to move, disconnect and secure your wheelchair. "It helps a lot if you have something written on your chair about your battery, and how to deal with the chair, in the language of the country you're going to," says Rosangela Berman-Beiler, a power chair user who has traveled repeatedly to several continents.

- Place labels and directions on your wheelchair, with information like whether your chair has a wet cell or dry cell battery, whether and how it can be folded or disassembled, the location of the quick disconnect terminals, how to set and release the brakes and any other special instructions.

- Make sure the airline puts a gate delivery tag on your wheelchair, so that it will be brought to you when you land, whether at your final destination, or when making connecting flights.

- Carry a set of tools as well as extra wires, fuses and other wheelchair parts which might need to be replaced upon arrival.

- Remove detachable and fragile parts from your wheelchair, and carry them with you onboard the plane.

- Disconnect the wheelchair battery yourself, or have your attendant do it, so that airline personnel will be less likely to try to do it themselves, potentially damaging something in the process.

- Put nametags on your wheelchair or other equipment, and on all removable parts.

Even more important than getting your wheelchair safely into the cargo hold, getting yourself aboard the plane may require careful planning and assertiveness. Always get to the airport early, and ask to board first. Be prepared to provide clear, simple directions about how to assist you onto the plane. "If you feel that the people who are helping you in the airplane don't know how to assist you, you have to tell them how you want to be helped," says Berman-Bieler. "Be in control in relation to your own body." If you cannot speak the same language as the airline assistants, ask for supervisors. Find someone who can translate for you; communication is key to safe, efficient transfers.

During an exchange program to Costa Rica, wheelchair user Tracee Garner learned some effective techniques for getting on and off the airplane with assistance. "Before I let the airline personnel begin to transfer me," says Garner, "I found it useful to be assertive and give brief instructions on how they could best assist me. I pointed a lot and used phrases such as, 'Grab here and not here,' or 'When you have my (legs, arms, etc.) you're going to move this way to get me here.' I made sure each person knew his or her role."

Other techniques for successful boarding with assistance include the following:

- Explain to the gate agent and to other personnel exactly what kind of help you will need—whether you need an aisle chair, whether you want to be lifted or can transfer yourself, whether you can walk onto the plane and how much support you will need.

- If possible, bring along your sliding board, transfer belt or other equipment you use to make transfers easier.

- Choose your travel attire carefully. Wear clothes that are loose enough to allow your body to move comfortably, but snug enough that they won't easily be pulled off! Says Garner: "I learned that wearing pants or shorts with tough material and a thick elastic waistband that can withstand pulling or has loops (jeans are perfect) provided a great place for a person to really get a good hold of and grab on to."

- Ask whether the aircraft has any seats with armrests that flip up, and request that seat assignment. If not, consider using a blanket to facilitate your transfer: Fold the blanket lengthwise over the airline seat, and over the armrests. Then the people assisting can have something to grab onto when lifting you into and out of the seat. In addition, the blanket can be used to scoot you back or reposition you during the flight.

- Learn your rights under the Air Carriers Access Act (ACAA), a federal law that governs U.S. airlines' treatment of travelers with disabilities. An airline may not refuse transportation to a passenger solely on the basis of a disability, nor limit the number of individuals with disabilities on a particular flight. The airline must transport mobility equipment, and cannot charge a fee for doing so. (The airline may require advance notice for transporting battery-powered wheelchairs, and may refuse if the aircraft is too small, i.e., if it has fewer than 30 seats.) Although the ACAA applies only to U.S. airlines, under a separate provision of the Federal Aviation Act, a foreign airline operating in the United States cannot participate in any unreasonable discrimination.

Whatever your disability, if you will need assistance getting through the airport or onto the airplane, think through and be ready to describe your needs. If you have a visual impairment, you may ask at check-in to have a sighted guide walk with you to the gate. Or if you feel that is unnecessary, you might ask for the gate agent to be alerted that you will be arriving soon, and to watch for you and arrange assistance as needed.

If you have a hidden disability, you will need to be particularly assertive and articulate in order to get prompt, appropriate assistance. If you have a respiratory or heart condition, chronic fatigue syndrome, arthritis, back pain or other disability that limits your mobility, you can ask to be transported to the gate in a wheelchair or electric cart.

If you have a respiratory condition and need to use supplemental oxygen, ask airlines about their policies before you book your flight. Some international carriers will provide therapeutic oxygen onboard the plane; others will not. (You cannot bring your own oxygen aboard any aircraft.) In order to have oxygen during the flight, you will have to request it in advance—usually 48 hours—and provide a letter from your doctor. Most airlines charge a fee for oxygen. Most will not provide oxygen on the ground, before or after your flight, or during layovers.

If you require the use of a ventilator to assist with breathing, you must work even more closely with the airline to plan to transport your equipment. Lori Hinderer, who uses 24-hour trach positive pressure ventilation due to muscular dystrophy, traveled to Lyon, France, to attend an international conference on home mechanical ventilation. She brought along two ventilators, so she would have an emergency backup during the long flight from St. Louis to Paris, and a non-spillable battery to power them. She arranged in advance for airline supervisors to meet her at each departing and returning connection, to assist her through customs and with connecting flights. There are also resources available that list ventilator service providers worldwide (see Appendix).

Access concerns do not end after you board. "Make sure to find out about whatever accessibility features are on the plane," advises Jean Marchant, who has multiple sclerosis—"whether there's a chair you can use on the plane and an accessible bathroom." Marchant also urges travelers with mobility impairments to research the facilities at any airports they will be traveling to or through. Marchant's trip to Germany included a stopover at London's Heathrow Airport. That stop turned out to be longer than expected. "Because of the noise pollution restrictions," Marchant explains, "our plane couldn't take off again; it was after 10 pm. So we were stuck there." Passengers were allowed to go into the airport to retrieve their bags but, says Marchant, the accessible bathroom was far from where they were, causing her discomfort. Using the Internet or the telephone, try to investigate the layout and access features of all of the airports along your route—even if you're only *expecting* a short layover—and consider possible contingency plans if access is unavailable. A bedpan or urinal in your carry-on luggage just might save the day!

Keeping track of your luggage can be another challenge of travel, especially if you are blind or visually impaired. "Mark your luggage so you can explain it to someone," suggests Frank Hernandez, who has traveled throughout Europe and also to Hong Kong. For example, decorate your suitcases with distinctive stickers or fasten a piece of tape or your favorite color yarn to their handles. Hernandez says that when he travels to another country, especially one where he does not speak the language fluently, he usually asks an airline official, rather than a local airport employee, to help him find his luggage.

A concern for some disabled travelers is maintaining a medication schedule when flying to distant time zones. Jean Marchant, who has multiple sclerosis, experienced an increase in her symptoms when she went to Germany, partly due to disruption of her medication regimen. "I was trying to adjust my medication, to keep it on a regular schedule, when I flew from the west coast to the east coast, and then to Europe," says Marchant. She tried to calculate the time differences, and to revise her medication schedule accordingly. "It would have been so much smarter just to set the alarm on my watch to go off every six to eight hours," she says now.

Airport security measures are another important factor to consider in making your trip overseas as smooth as possible. Security screening is particularly rigorous for international flights. Before going to the airport, you should find out how the screening process may interact with your disability and your equipment. In most cases, screening procedures can be adapted based on your needs. Consult the Appendix for information and guidelines on airport security.

Getting Around

Navigating in a less than accessible or unfamiliar environment may be difficult for people with different kinds of disabilities who go abroad. Rather than being an obstacle, the challenge of getting around in a new place simply demands adaptation and creative problem-solving.

People with cognitive impairments or learning disabilities, for example, can develop appropriate strategies for finding their way around. One college student shared that she was worried about getting lost and not being able to process directions given to her verbally. She found it helped to have information, such as directions, typed or written down. The skills she learned as a result of the time she spent abroad helped her to better advocate for herself when she returned home.

Carefully consider what *you* need in order to find your way through an unfamiliar city. You may do better with written directions; or with auditory directions recorded on a portable tape player; or perhaps with pictoral maps, or with another person whom you feel comfortable assisting or accompanying you. Other students or staff on the exchange program or disability organizations in the host country could provide this assistance, if arranged beforehand. Go prepared to advocate for yourself, and to make whatever

Prepare as well as you can but do not be attached to your plans. If you hang on tightly to your plans, you may end up feeling frustrated and perhaps angry and resentful toward the people, culture, systems and structures of your host country.

arrangements will work best for you in your new environment. Keep in mind that things will often not be like what you are used to at home, and you'll need to think creatively and be flexible to address new access issues that might arise.

If you are with an exchange group, make sure your leaders and your co-travelers understand your needs, whatever they may be. When Silia Herrera traveled to Costa Rica with Mobility International USA, her cerebral palsy, which affects the right side of her body, slowed her down—but only a little. She wears a leg brace and, she says, her biggest concerns about traveling revolved around possible difficulties with navigating stairs and walking long distances. "I just took one day at a time, and adapted to each situation appropriately," she says. Other group members had access issues, too, which varied according to their disabilities. "We basically accommodated each others' needs," she says.

Blind people experience different kinds of navigation concerns. "Mobility is very different in other parts of the world than it is here [in the United States]," says Jean Parker, who is blind. She has spent a great deal of time in India where, she says, "There are no sidewalks, and everyone is in the road together—pedestrians, motorcycles, trucks, buses, rickshaws." Moving without sight through such a river of humanity and machinery, Parker says, sometimes necessitates asking strangers for assistance. "You have to get help more than you would [at home], so you just have to reconcile yourself to that." Fortunately, getting help is relatively easy there. "You're never alone when you're in India," she explains. "It's very easy to get somebody's attention. People who see a blind person will make contact" and offer help.

Many disabled travelers offer similar reports about many different countries, especially less-industrialized countries. By being open to accepting help, many disabled travelers agree, you are more likely to learn practical approaches to overcoming barriers, and to come away with a cross-cultural experience. "Don't be afraid of asking for help," says Alicia Contreras, a Mexican woman who has navigated many parts of the world, from China to Kenya to Nicaragua, in her manual wheelchair. "The reality is that when things are not accessible, there are two options—just don't do those things, or ask somebody for help. I think that's important to learn."

Understanding different cultural concepts of independence is crucial for the disabled traveler. In the United States and many other Western countries, independence often means moving and functioning without any help from other people. In developing countries, where fewer resources are available for assistive technology and full accessibility, disabled people achieve independence *with* help from others. Travelers who are able to recognize their own internalized values and adapt to new situations are more likely to get around effectively.

By being creative, you may find ways to navigate difficult environments, and perhaps minimize the amount of assistance you will need. When you encounter unramped sidewalks, you may be able to use side streets and driveway entrances. When you have to use streets with no sidewalks, consider adjusting your schedule to travel through those areas when there's less traffic. Or if possible, take taxis, which may be relatively inexpensive in many countries.

If you come from a developing country, you may be surprised, at first, to find an apparent reluctance to help others among people living in more industrialized nations. Try to keep an open mind and recognize the variety of responses you may encounter as time goes on, and the value of doing things on your own. Many people are, in fact, quite helpful. Learn to assess when asking for help is culturally appropriate, and when it is not. And take advantage of access features (when available) like lifts on buses, ramped sidewalks, power wheelchairs, adaptive computers, closed captioning, universal signage and audible signals. Independent living centers or other disability organizations may be able to rent or lend you adaptive equipment, provide technology training, or assist you with orientation to accessible systems, such as training in using wheelchair lift-equipped buses.

As Karla Rivas, who studied as a Fulbright fellow in the United States, noted about the assistive technology she received, "I started to become very independent: writing my papers and doing everything myself. That helped me a lot. Also, I got my books on tape from the Library of Congress' National Library Service for the Blind." Outside of campus, she also found assistance in the community. "Sometimes at first I was afraid, but you find ways to do things. People, when they see you, they help you. I cooked for myself, but my friends took me once a month to the supermarket. I tried to buy everything I needed for the month when I went. It worked well for me," Rivas said. "Also I got a service from an independent living center so all my clothes are labeled with Braille. I can match my clothes now without having to ask others."

Likewise, travelers from developed countries, depending on their destination and disability type, may need to shift their expectations regarding access, and to ask for and accept help when needed. If you are coming from a place where you are accustomed to being independent in a reasonably accessible world, you may hesitate to approach strangers to ask for help. Once you accept the necessity of doing so, how do you do it? "You just watch," says Mary Lou Breslin, a wheelchair user who has coped with unramped curbs and inaccessible transportation on several continents. "On a busy street there's a lot of people. People walking down the street notice you. People immediately try to be helpful. [In countries where there is little access] helping people is kind of a regular, everyday thing. It's really easy to get help. You gesture, get their attention, and then point to yourself, point to the street, smile, do motions with your hands." Learning some basic words and phrases in the host country's language will also be helpful and appreciated.

Assistance with navigation can pose its own problems when it comes uninvited and unwanted. Don Galloway, who is blind, has found his way through many African and Caribbean countries. He does ask for help sometimes, but he prefers to rely on his cane and his mobility skills. Especially in Africa, Galloway found that "people have a tendency to grab you more, to get into your private space more. It was hard for me to deal with their assistance." He respectfully asserted his self-sufficiency. "I would say, 'No, I have a cane.' I would be as polite as possible, and tell them I didn't need this." Eventually people began recognizing his competence. "After a while, they started seeing that I could get around. And they were delighted. Here's a blind guy who can get around by himself!"

Strangers need not be the only source of help with getting around in a foreign city. People with disabilities similar to yours, who have experience navigating in the locale, can teach you. When Galloway was the Peace Corps country director in Jamaica, he contacted the Jamaica Society for the Blind. The friends he met there became his guides and mentors. "I would go into the streets and use my cane with them. I would be walking past goats and cows. If I was by myself, it would have been really strange. But having someone there helped a lot." Galloway recommends reaching out to local disabled people, as he did. "Choose somebody who is aggressive and knows how to get around the society," he says. Similarly, people who are Deaf often find it useful to connect with local Deaf organizations to learn the country's sign language, social opportunities and available services.

Friends with and without disabilities can help you get around more effectively in foreign places, Jean Parker agrees. "Generally it's much safer to travel with people who know the country—and more efficient." Local contacts can help navigate not just geographically, but also culturally. "There are things that might be apparent to a sighted person, that might not be readily obvious to me as a blind person," says Parker. "If somebody is there to give me information and clues about what's going on and why, it makes traveling much more interesting and more fun, and it makes getting to know people much easier."

You may be surprised to discover that getting around in a new city is not as hard as you may have expected. Sarah Presley, who is blind, lived in Morocco for two years as a Peace Corps Volunteer. Learning to navigate meant relying on skills and strategies she had learned at home. "My confidence grew as I found that I could get around Rabat without too much difficulty," Presley says. "I found that the same method that I used in unfamiliar settings in the U.S.—that is, becoming familiar with the areas around my house and job and then branching out—worked just as well in Morocco. I just had to be a little more careful of potholes! In some ways, getting from one place to another was easier for me in Rabat than it is in most cities in the United States, because fewer people have cars, so there is more public transportation."

As many travelers point out, access barriers are definitely an issue for people with mobility impairments who venture abroad.

Europe can be particularly difficult, with its centuries-old buildings and long stairways. Those were precisely the buildings that student Robin Tovey was interested in visiting during a school trip to France. Tovey was born without arms or legs and uses a motorized wheelchair. Passionately interested in French culture and art, Tovey took every opportunity to go to museums, cathedrals, palaces and other historical locations. She learned to ask questions about access features in these places. "Some buildings have elevators (or other compensations) and some do not," says Tovey. "Most often employees knew the accessibility situation and were up-front and often apologetically honest about their inaccessibility." Occasionally, Tovey was pleasantly surprised at the alternative access arrangements that were made available to her. For example, at the Chateau de Versailles, the home of King Louis XIV, main entrances were completely inaccessible. Instead, says Tovey, "we got to go behind the scenes to a serviceable, yet semi-industrial, elevator."

If you are planning a longer stay in one location, for school or a long-term volunteer assignment, you may need more regular and reliable access to some buildings—or some reasonable alternative. Vanessa Jones, a wheelchair user, spent two years at the University of London's Courtauld Institute, obtaining a Master's degree in art history. She found accessibility at the Institute to be "reasonable, though not complete," with a ramped side entrance, an elevator, and a wheelchair-accessible bathroom. The second floor in the library could only be reached from a flight of stairs but, says Jones, "the librarians were always happy to bring down any resources I needed."

Transportation

Transportation, whether public or private, is particularly important and can be problematic. Barriers can make getting around difficult for people with all kinds of mobility impairments, but willing helping hands can often make up for a lack of access. Jean Lin has cerebral palsy and uses crutches or, sometimes, a wheelchair. During a three-week exchange program in Russia, Lin had to make frequent decisions about what kinds of transportation to use. Taxis were easiest, but expensive. Most affordable was the subway, but it contained "a lot of physical barriers," says Lin. "We had to be open to waving down people to help us get down the stairs." Many passersby would willingly provide assistance. "Everybody was very friendly and helpful," Lin recalls.

If transportation turns out to be a stumbling block—if the typical options are not too accessible, or are unreliable or hazardous— one option is to make private or specialized arrangements that will meet your needs. Alicia Contreras has sometimes hired a full-time driver to transport her and her wheelchair, as well as other members of her group. "I would prefer to hire someone who will ask for more money. Or I will pay a taxi cab, which is more expensive than public transportation." Contreras feels these choices give her more control over her schedule and her safety. In London, Vanessa Jones found the available public transportation (the Underground and the city buses) to be generally inaccessible. "Wheelchair users can use the accessible taxis, which have ramps and do not require one to get out of one's wheelchair, but these are expensive," Jones says. "Special door-to-door transportation services for people with disabilities are available, but these often proved unreliable." Jones decided to make her own arrangements. "I decided to buy a car fitted with hand controls, which I then resold at the end of my stay." This offered the additional advantage of giving Jones "the freedom to leave the city on weekends and visit outlying areas." She applied for a permit which allowed her to park in metered spaces for several hours without paying.

Some countries offer international drivers licenses, so check with the department of motor vehicles or transportation in the country you are traveling to, to see if this option is available. Many countries, however, do not grant driver's licenses to foreigners and most exchange programs do not allow participants to drive abroad. And many disabled travelers find public transportation to be quite satisfactory. Susan Sygall, a manual wheelchair user and frequent world traveler, took local buses in Guatemala, Malaysia and Thailand with the help of a friend. She also suggests bringing your adaptive bike if this is common transportation in the city. Again, the keys to success include careful advance research and planning, and contacts with local disabled people who can help you navigate through the transportation systems.

While studying in Italy, Donna Cencer wanted to see as much of the country as she could. Seeking affordable, rea-

The value of planning ahead lies not in making sure that everything will be set up for you, but in opening your mind to imagine the experience you will have. It gives you an opportunity to learn about the country you'll be visiting and to think about ways you will address potential barriers before facing them. It also allows you to explore available resources (counseling, Braille, wheelchair repair, pharmacy, etc.) before you need them. Once you arrive, you can draw on this information. If something you had set up falls through, you'll have a backup plan.

sonably accessible transportation, she discovered trains. "Traveling by train in Italy is easy and inexpensive for students, assuming there are no labor strikes," she says. Cencer has a mobility impairment and needed some help boarding the trains. "Most Italian people are willing to help lift baggage onto the train or offer other physical assistance, but it was important for me to be assertive and let people know that I needed assistance and how they could best help me."

Mary Lou Breslin is a wheelchair user who has experienced a wide range of transportation systems. In Tokyo, she says, "We took the subway all over the city. There are only a few accessible stations that have elevators." The other stations, Breslin says, "had dramatic ways to get you up and down the stairs." Several stations, for example, used stair climbing devices. In another station, a wheelchair would be leaned way back and strapped onto a platform, which would then move slowly up the stairs on a tread, somewhat like a tank. In yet another station, a stair lift is part of the escalator. "They stop the escalator, get everyone off, and you get on," Breslin reports. "The lift activates, and music begins to play in the background, and the music is 'Home, Home on the Range'! It's a big deal; several people have to activate this thing." Some stations had no such fancy equipment and instead, Breslin says, "I got carried up and down the stairs in my motorized wheelchair. Six men would come out and hoist it up!"

Breslin adds, "We took cabs in Bosnia and buses in Russia. I got lifted onto the buses in Russia—the driver or somebody just steps up to the plate." To cope successfully in a foreign environment often means adapting to imperfect infrastructure, and accepting human help. Although Breslin describes herself as "a person with a disability who's completely committed to doing things independently," she says she has to adjust her attitude when she travels.

"You cannot have the attitude that, 'This bus doesn't have a lift, so I'm not going to get on it.' You really have to let go of that, and decide it's okay to be lifted. And I was, over and over again. You just do it the way everybody does it when you're there."

Historian Anatoli Ilyashov traveled to Russia as a Fulbright scholar. He has multiple sclerosis, and used a cane during his trip. Ilyashov had to contend with fatigue as well as restricted mobility. "As time went on, the Russian people were great in accommodating me," he says. "They were conscious of my situation and often helped me into buses, trams and trolley cars. One of my biggest concerns was procuring less exhausting, more reliable forms of transportation when I needed to get to a doctor or when I was simply too tired to deal with the daily trolley ride. The Fulbright liaison and my fellow faculty members were very supportive and helpful in this. My transportation concerns were always worked out. Creativity, a willingness to explore all possible resources and the ability to clearly communicate your needs are key."

Safety

Moving around in an unfamiliar environment may also involve safety risks that should be addressed. Street crimes including mugging and pickpocketing are concerns for international travelers, especially those visiting crowded urban areas. Disabled people may feel particularly at risk of such crimes, because of reduced mobility, vision or hearing. Or, some suggest, you may be safer, because more people may be watching you. The travelers who gave input for this book offered several safety strategies, which are valid for people both with and without disabilities, including the following.

- Try not to appear an easy target. Move confidently and with purpose, especially if you use an adaptive tool such as a white cane, crutches or a wheelchair for your mobility.

- Learn about the neighborhoods you will be traveling through, and which neighborhoods to avoid. In addition to information about which neighborhoods are considered dangerous, disabled travelers should also consider factors which may interfere with their orientation or mobility—factors such as inadequate street lighting, access barriers, and poorly maintained streets and sidewalks.

- In particularly dangerous areas, avoid being alone; ask a friend to go with you—especially a local, someone who knows the territory.

- Keep your money, credit cards and other valuables well hidden. *Don't* keep your purse or wallet on the back of your wheelchair or on your walker or crutches! Instead, conceal your cash in or under your wheelchair seat, or wear a money belt.

- Make copies of your travel documents, such as passport and visas, and keep the originals separate in a secure place.

- Know how to contact your country's embassy or consulate wherever you are. If you are Deaf, find out how to contact these officials by TTY, email or fax.

- Bring along international telephone information, such as dialing codes, so you will know how to reach your home country from wherever you are.

Women with disabilities should be aware of additional hazards such as possible gender-based violence and harassment. Tanis Doe, who is Deaf and a wheelchair user, explains, "Unaccompanied women in male-dominated countries may be vulnerable." Research attitudes toward women with disabilities in particular, so you'll know what to expect. Also consider getting in contact with organizations in the host country that work specifically on issues related to women with disabilities. (See the Appendix for resources to locate such organizations.) Doe's advice is to "not be alone and to have people around you who are from that culture or country."

Depending on where you plan to travel, you may also need to think about being safe from political or general violence. North Americans are becoming more aware of the potential dangers, but residents of some countries have lived with this reality for years—and so have international travelers. How can you incorporate into your travel plans the possibility—however remote— that you will witness or be affected by political unrest? First, take reasonable precautions: Pay attention to travel advisories issued by your government, seek the counsel of local exchange staff and hosts, and follow current events in the countries you will visit. Adjust your level of caution or risk-taking accordingly. Be aware of your surroundings in airports and in crowded areas.

Next, educate yourself about political situations and their roots, so that you can keep the dangers in perspective, and talk intelligently about and develop responses to it. "I'm pretty in tune to the attitudes toward our government" among peoples around the world, says Jenny Kern, a wheelchair user from the United States. Since politics can become the topic of discussion in some settings, it would be helpful to be able to talk about your country's policies on different subjects and be open to learning about the host country's policies. Also, if you visit a volatile area, make safety a part of your process of settling in. Study the safety and evacuation plans of your hotel or apartment. Figure out an accessible escape route, or know who you can call on in the event of emergency.

Making Connections

When you go abroad in a group or delegation, chances are you will have more companionship than you know what to do with! If you travel alone, however, especially for an extended period of time, you may find yourself feeling lonely. Isolation can be a fairly common experience for many international travelers, with and without disabilities. Entering an environment where you don't know anyone, and where the language, customs, streets and food are unfamiliar, you may develop a sense of loneliness. Some disabled people find that negative attitudes, staring, inaccessible transportation and communication barriers make it even harder to develop connections in a new place.

Even in a group, you can sometimes feel alone. If you are the only disabled person in your group, you may find yourself struggling with feeling different, stigmatized or left out. Your fellow group members and other people you meet might not know how to react to your wheelchair; or you might be the only Deaf person among people who do not know sign language. Or perhaps you are afraid to share the fact that you have a psychiatric history, HIV or epilepsy. Carole Patterson, former project manager of the National Clearinghouse on Disability and Exchange, writes, "Exchange participants may encounter the isolation that comes from being different, from being… in the minority, whether due to disability, race, ethnicity, sexual orientation, religion or a combination of these attributes."

Isolation can feel like a burden at times, but even this aspect of traveling can pay off with valuable new perspectives. Heather Harker, who is Deaf and has traveled to many remote locations, says, "The worst times were when I struggled with loneliness, frustration and sheer exhaustion from always being with people of another culture. However," Harker adds, "I gained confidence, skills in communicating with individuals from different cultures and with different languages, an understanding of what it is like to be a minority all the time and a heightened sense of self-knowledge." Many people who go on exchanges find that they grow to enjoy being with people from different cultures.

If things seem difficult within your group at first, don't give up. Awkwardness and even prejudice can be transcended with sincere effort and openness. Alan Shain volunteered with Youth Challenge International, a Canadian organization, to work in remote areas of Costa Rica. Shain uses a walker and has a speech impairment. He was the only person with a mobility disability in the multinational group of fourteen people who worked together to build a dormitory out of prefabricated material. "The issue of being seen as a full participant of the group at the same time as needing physical support was difficult to overcome," says Shain. "I often had to be especially vocal to ensure I was included when responsibilities were being delegated. The more outgoing I was in taking on different duties, the more the group accepted me as a co-worker, and with that came less of a focus on the assistance I needed to get around."

How can you address the feelings that sometimes arise from the experience of being alone in a foreign country? "I would encourage people to know about disability groups in other countries," says David Oaks, a frequent traveler who has been diagnosed with a psychiatric disability. "The highlight of some of my trips has been visiting drop-in centers, having dinner together and feeling connected."

Meeting disabled people in the countries you visit offers practical benefits, as discussed before, but it can also be an important source of companionship and emotional support. Finding these connections might take some work, but the rewards may be well worth the effort. The following are some ways that travelers with disabilities have made contacts in local disability communities overseas.

- Find disability organizations by contacting Disabled Peoples' International, the World Blind Union, the World Federation of the Deaf, Support Coalition International or other global groups, such as disabled sports or women's organizations, and ask them for local contacts and resources.

- Visit schools, grassroots advocacy organizations, independent living centers or rehabilitation centers where you might meet people with disabilities.

- Meet people through the Internet, using caution and discretion of course. There are disability chat forums and message boards where you might connect with people.

- Be friendly. You might meet disabled people in public places or through friends. While not everyone will be open to an overture from a complete stranger, some people will—especially if you approach them with warmth and respect.

See the Appendix for information about more resources overseas, compiled by the National Clearinghouse on Disability and Exchange.

Finally, don't forget your usual connections. You may find you still need the affection and support of family and friends back home. Write letters, or if you have access to a computer, stay in touch through electronic mail. You may find that you need to specifically ask your loved ones to write back to you. When Susan Brown was struggling with depression during her Peace Corps service in Ukraine, she reached out to her friends back home, but rarely received responses. "I tried to help them understand and they didn't get it," says Brown. "So my friends didn't write and they rarely called." She knows they were busy, and intended to stay in touch but didn't want to disappoint her with only a brief message. "That short email would help a lot," Brown says. Her advice to other travelers: "Make sure that the people that you leave behind understand how important it is for them to maintain their support while you're over there."

Communication

Making contacts and feeling connected depend partly upon your ability to communicate with the people around you. That doesn't mean, however, that you have to put off traveling until you become fluent in one or more foreign languages. Many travelers have found language to be less of an obstacle than they anticipated. Silvia Gutierrez' first trip outside the United States was a short-term program to Russia. "Despite the language barrier, my host sister and I hit it off right from the start," recalls Gutierrez. "I remember we always understood each other—laughing and gesturing our way through dinner and our evenings together. The ability to transcend different languages is a gift I'll treasure the rest of my life each time I encounter a difficult situation in human relations."

On the other hand, if you plan to stay in a country longer than a few weeks, seriously consider studying the local language before and/or during your trip. Having a disability, you may face barriers in your new temporary home; don't let your inability to speak the language become yet another barrier. When Sarah Presley served in the Peace Corps, learning Moroccan Arabic was crucial to her adapting to the country. "Because I am not able to see people's gestures and facial expressions, I found that learning the language and learning it fast was an absolute necessity," she explains. For those using personal assistants in the host country, you will also find a solid language base is essential for training and instruction. It will also help you to improve your language skills by having someone local to communicate with on a daily basis.

If you have a disability that affects your hearing, speech or learning processes, there are other aspects for which to plan. As a participant in an exchange program sponsored by the University of Florida, David Dye traveled to Rio de Janeiro, Brazil. A year later he embarked on a year-long program at Brazil's Universidade de São Paulo. Because of his hearing loss, Dye had some difficulty mastering Portuguese, but he worked hard and was able to gain proficiency. "My ability to understand Portuguese developed more slowly than my ability to speak the language," says Dye. "Often during my first few months in Brazil, people would assume that because I spoke well, I was just as good at understanding what they were saying. Wrong. I always became confused when the other person responded. 'Como?' ('What?') became an essential word in my vocabulary at the time. But I never gave in to frustration; instead I persevered. By the end of my year I understood 90 percent of what I heard. Because my level of understanding decreases if I'm not watching the other person's lips the whole time, I had to educate people about what I needed to have a successful conversation."

Even if the language is the same as yours, accents may make lip reading difficult. Sarah Beauchamp, who is Deaf and traveled to Scotland as a university student, shares the initial frustrations she had upon arrival: "Once in Scotland, it took only a short time to make me think I had made a serious mistake. I had a difficult time understanding people—Scottish people certainly have thick, heavy accents! My years of speech therapy and learning to lip read—on Americans—were practically useless. It was the most frustrating experience. However, I was glad to go through it, because I felt it made me more determined to challenge myself throughout my life."

If you feel your disability will make learning a language more difficult, give yourself as many advantages as you can: Start studying the language as far in advance as possible. Hire a tutor, or ask your school to provide one for you. Be willing, like Dye, to educate the people you meet about your communication style and needs. Finally, be patient with yourself; trust that the more time you spend immersed in the culture, the more your language skills will improve.

Having a significant hearing impairment may actually convey a cross-cultural communication advantage, because it means being part of a global Deaf community. Daisy Sipp, a Deaf woman who spent sixteen days on an exchange in Costa Rica, says that Deaf people may have an advantage in overcoming language barriers: "Deaf people can use gestures because they are already part of our language." Sipp can read the lips of English-speakers, but she does not speak Spanish. In Costa Rica, "I had to use lot of gestures and facial expressions," she says.

Where major language differences exist, interpreters can help to overcome communication barriers. In a multi-lingual encounter, conversation can become complicated, sometimes amusingly so. Sipp's group spoke several languages among them, including English, Spanish and several varieties of sign language. Each group member had a chance to be group leader for one day. The day when Sipp was the leader happened to be media day, when several reporters came to conduct interviews. "We had to have three translations: I signed to the American Sign Language interpreter, then she voiced for me. Then the Spanish interpreter had to listen to my interpreter and translate it to Spanish. It was awesome! But of course, it took some time." The reporters were confused at first, Sipp says. "We had to explain it to them over and over," until they finally understood the process. "After that they smiled and became more curious about our program," says Sipp.

While knowing foreign languages is extremely helpful, it's not always possible. If you travel frequently to different countries, or if a travel opportunity arises suddenly, you may not be able to master the language before you arrive. Then you'll have to rely on interpreters—a situation which requires its own kind of skill and assertiveness, as you negotiate systems and events. "If you don't know the language, you'd better be listening to what's going on, so that someone isn't changing things without bothering to let you know about it," says Jean Parker. At such times, she tries to take charge. "I just stop the conversation. I say, 'Hey, I have the feeling you're talking about something that regards me, and I would ask that you include me in that discussion.'"

Cultural Interactions

Anyone who travels internationally will encounter cultural differences—customs, beliefs, values and habits that may diverge slightly or significantly from one's home environment. For disabled travelers, disability itself can be a site of cultural dissonance. The results of this dissonance may be either conflict and discomfort, or acceptance and personal growth—depending on your willingness and ability to come to terms with foreign cultural ideas and practices. Keep an open mind about other people's attitudes and ways of doing things, and about your own cultural assumptions. Be aware of your own reactions to new situations, and work to transform those reactions into new understanding.

You will come face-to-face with all kinds of cultural differences, some conceptual and some concrete. "Bathrooms are tough," says Frank Hernandez, a world traveler who is blind. "In Europe, no two bathrooms are alike!" he jokes. European toilets have many different kinds of flushing mechanisms—including chains, cranks, recessed buttons and other kinds of controls—and all in different locations. All of this can make it difficult for a non-European, especially one with a visual impairment, to do what needs to be done. Hernandez recommends the straightforward, inquisitive approach. Asking questions, and acting on the information you receive will help you come to grips with many of the specific cultural differences you run across.

In addition to the details of how things work, you will also discover philosophies that may be at odds with your own belief system. How you receive this information, and how you choose to interact with the culture, will have a major impact on your experience abroad.

Pamela Houston, who has cerebral palsy that affects her walking and other movements, served as a Peace Corps Volunteer in the Republic of Kiribati, a small Pacific island nation. She was somewhat dismayed by the country's attitudes and images about people with disabilities. "There is stigma and shame attached to being disabled that comes from a belief that one's disability is caused by that person or his/her immediate family having done something wrong, by black magic or by some ancestral sin," says Houston. "The weight of cultural attitudes and the deeper underlying stigma results in people with disabilities often seeing themselves and being seen as helpless and as burdens to their families. Many are kept hidden and are not given opportunities to participate in community life. Even the disabled people themselves, including those who were organizing for change within their communities, tended to frame their issues in fairly negative ways. In working with these organizers, Houston offered her own perspectives, urging and modeling more positive views. Yet she recognized that they were making slow but steady progress. Houston challenged herself to recognize this progress, and the potential for change within the community. She made herself take a lower profile, while the disabled people of Kiribati expressed their problems and their hopes in their own terms. "I had to let go of needing the message to meet with my Western, disability rights-bearing philosophy," Houston says.

Different cultures deal with disabilities in many different ways. Even in so-called advanced countries, people with disabilities have not yet achieved full equality. In particular, people from the United States need to be careful about labeling another country as backward or "way behind America" simply because of perceived negative attitudes and/or physical barriers. Your experiences will not reflect the totality of the disability experience in that culture. For instance, in some countries, people with disabilities are used to services being provided by the government, or hiring outside assistance; in other countries or even in different cultures within the same country, the family or community provides these services when needed. Different doesn't mean inferior.

There is always more to the story than what you as a foreigner might observe. For example, when Tanis Doe went to Jamaica, she sensed discomfort among the Jamaicans regarding both her deafness and her physical disability, which requires her to use a wheelchair. "People stared at me and felt nervous around me," she recalls. Doe looked deeper, however. "In the families of people with disabilities," she discovered, "there was a positive role for disabled children and adults. Even if society did not fully accept them, their family seemed very supportive. This included people with developmental disabilities as well as Deaf and mentally ill people. It was harder for people with physical disabilities since there was little access in the rural areas, and no public transit. But despite the fear and difficulty with dealing with disability they seemed to care for their children well."

Your cultural perspective may impact your perception of the things you experience abroad. For example, if you are an American like Jean Parker, trained in mobility and other blindness skills, you are accustomed to walking independently. Parker found that in India, however, "if you're there with a cane, and you look like you're crossing a road, someone will help you. In the United States, you might be offended by that. But," Parker adds, "the cultural motivation is different. In many places, people who have disabilities, the only way they are visible is as beggars, or as street musicians, or somehow in a role different from what we know. So, the people you come into contact with have only seen disabled people in that role." By your very presence, and by your active participation in your exchange program or profession, you will be challenging those perceptions. Parker adds, "There's a separation that happens, where people will accept you as an exception to the usual roles of disabled people because you're a foreigner." She admits this is frustrating, especially to someone who believes passionately in all people's equality. "Some things you can't win," says Parker. "That's probably one of them."

Alicia Contreras agrees. "There's no way to change anyone, if they don't want to be changed," she says. "I have learned that we really have to be very respectful of each culture." Doing otherwise can make your travels more difficult than they need to be, by leading you to set unrealistic expectations. Contreras is a Mexican woman, now living in the United States, who uses a wheelchair. She has traveled with groups of disabled people, in which some North Americans "were expecting accessible transportation, and to have ramps everywhere. People were expecting to have every single thing they had back home. Those people were miserable!" On the other hand, says Contreras, people who accepted and respected other cultures "had a much better opportunity to enjoy the trip." For people who cannot accept those differences, Contreras has this advice: "If you want to be comfortable just like at home, stay at home"—or choose to go to countries with similar access and accommodations.

If you push yourself outside your cultural comfort zone, and open yourself to learning more about the world—and about yourself— you will be well-equipped to be a cross-cultural traveler. Cross-cultural conversations often become the most vivid memories treasured by returning exchange participants. Sarah Presley, who is blind, volunteered for the Peace Corps and worked as a teacher at a school for the blind in Rabat, Morocco. She and her students enjoyed talking with each other at length, on subjects both serious and lighthearted. "We had many discussions about the situation of blind people in the United States and in Morocco," Presley says. "Sometimes we argued about such things as whether blind people should use canes and whether it is necessary for blind students to learn contracted Braille. Usually, though, we just talked about life in general and laughed a lot."

Anatoli Ilyashov traveled to Russia as a Fulbright scholar. He has a mobility impairment resulting from multiple sclerosis. "Culti-vate patience with yourself, your learning process and the folks who will populate your new life," Ilyashov advises. "Practice respect," he adds. "Learn how people think and integrate what you have to give with their way of viewing the world." Ilyashov believes these strategies will work for all international travelers, disabled and nondisabled alike. "People with disabilities participating in exchanges have additional roles," states Ilyashov. "We build bridges (as do all good international delegates) and we break down barriers for others with disabilities."

Jessica Aaron had the chance to be such a bridge-builder when she spent three weeks and then a semester studying in Mexico on exchanges. "We discussed the importance of access and disability awareness with the mayor of Tepic, Nayarit," she recalls. "We also addressed a group of architecture students at a local university on the meaning of access and why buildings should be made accessible when they are constructed. The cultural sharing between the U.S. group and the Mexican disability community was also valuable. I spoke to other people with disabilities about my life in the United States—my job, my power wheelchair, my education in a school where children with and

Communication is key. People, whether they are airline staff, exchange coordinators or passersby on the street, aren't going to know how they can assist you if you don't tell them clearly and respectfully. Remember that when you are communicating in another language, no matter how well you know that language, there is a large cultural gap between what you think you are saying and what the hearer thinks you are saying. Be patient and listen carefully to responses so you can learn how to communicate more effectively.

without disabilities learned together, and the accessible streets and public transportation in my home town. I hoped to help them imagine their lives in a world where they had equal rights and opportunities. At the same time, I shared with them my difficulties in the United States, such as some inaccessible buildings and transportation, and the attitudinal barriers to access." Attitudes of local exchange staff also changed as Aaron worked with them to solve access issues, such as removing doors to add extra inches of space to allow her wheelchair to fit into bathrooms or classrooms. Along with her strong Spanish skills, she gradually learned the local etiquette for greeting people in the community, which helped her to gain acceptance. Hiring and training a local personal assistant also gave her community connections apart from the university, and enriched her cultural experience.

Your cultural perspective, and your ability to respect others' cultural perspectives, will be especially important when you travel abroad to collaborate with foreign partners. Whether your role is to be a student, an adviser, a teacher or volunteer, you will be most successful if you can avoid ethnocentrism—that is, a presumption that your ethnic or cultural framework is superior to others. Don Galloway is a blind man from the United States, who has lent technical assistance to disability groups in Europe, Africa and the Caribbean. "We had a lot to offer," Galloway says, "but we needed to listen to what those in the host country are about. They wanted to share in our philosophy, but they didn't want to be dictated to. You can't say, 'This is the way you do it.' Because that may *not* be the best way for them, based on their social and economic history." This doesn't mean that you don't have a valid viewpoint, and important contributions to make. Your counterparts in other countries will likely "look upon meeting you as an opportunity to share information and ideas and make linkages," says Galloway.

Just keep your viewpoint and your contribution in perspective. The knowledge you have is valuable but limited by your particular background. Also, if you are coming from a richer country, and wanting to be of service to people in poorer countries, it is important to understand the historical relations among richer and poorer countries. It's equally important to be aware of your own motives. Canadian Tanis Doe, who has been involved in international disability work, says that she is very aware of her privilege. When working with people in other countries, Doe tries to share her skills in a way that allows people to increase the tools they have available to better their lives on their own terms. This philosophy is echoed by Heather Harker, an American Deaf woman who worked in Malaysia with the Deaf community for a year and a half. "In Malaysia I learned that people themselves must be the agents of change," says Harker. "Otherwise it is not actually an empowering change. The Deaf community in Malaysia taught me a great deal about how change is created and how a community can overcome barriers with innovation and persistence." Reaping the reward of wisdom is one of the bonuses of overseas travel—and it depends heavily on approaching other cultures with humility and respect, and on transferring knowledge and expertise.

Travelers who have experienced discrimination and poverty at home, may be surprised to find that in another country you may be regarded as privileged and affluent by people both with and without disabilities. This relates to an important cultural lesson: While disability does have a major impact on the lives of people around the world, economics have an even bigger impact. Don Galloway found that throughout the developing world, he was more or less protected from the negative attitudes directed at local blind people. "They see that you are an affluent person, because you dress well and so on," says Galloway. "They treat you better than they do their own people with disabilities. It's more of an economic thing than a disability thing." For example, Galloway noted that in Zimbabwe, men with all types of disabilities have little chance of getting married, because of the assumption that they cannot work and support a family. On the other hand, Galloway found that as an African-American man, many women were drawn to him regardless of his blindness. In many countries, disabled Americans are assumed to be relatively wealthy, powerful and independent based on their country of origin, as well as their ability to travel. "'You got here, so you must have some income,'" is the attitude, according to Galloway.

On the other hand, the disability can help to offset some of the imbalance that typically exists between citizens of richer and poorer countries. Jenny Kern, a wheelchair user, finds that "in East Africa, the people are surprised to see a white person with a disability. I think it makes me more equal to people, because they see that I'm not privileged." *Sometimes*, that is. "On the other hand," Kern adds, "it depends on people's attitudes and what seems to trump what. If you have money to fly, we're not going to give you a hard time at customs. Or, you're a disabled person so we need to handle you with extra care and be overprotective." In other words, navigating a different cultural landscape can be complicated. "It's so hard to know, in any given interaction, what's coming into play."

With so many unknown cultural variables, how will you know when your disability has become a point of contention? And how should you respond? "In general," Kern says, "I try to be low-key and respectful." However, Kern says she will be assertive when it's needed.

You may also encounter all kinds of differences in resolving issues abroad. For example, in the United States, privacy is a highly valued and closely guarded right. But in other societies, where people think more about the collective well-being than about individual concerns, confidentiality doesn't have the same relevance. In such societies, groups and communities discuss solutions for people's problems collectively. This can be an especially important practice of which visitors and local people with disabilities should be aware.

Some U.S.-based travelers find it quite welcoming to visit countries whose societies more clearly take this approach. When Harriet Johnson spent time in Cuba, she was moved by the natural acceptance which she felt from acquaintances and strangers alike. Johnson, a wheelchair user, was impressed by the way passersby offered assistance without making a fuss. "Throughout the day people help, and it's never a big deal," she wrote during her trip to Cuba. "It's hard to pin down, but here I get the feeling that being disabled is no big deal." Although she observed poverty and hardship, Johnson discovered that the Cubans she met had already learned what the civil and social movements try to teach— that we are all in this together. Johnson found that it clearly influenced the way she was treated. "People talk to me," she says. "In my hometown, strangers tend to address my nondisabled companions, not me. In Havana, I'm treated as more of a person."

Your cultural experiences will depend partly on your approach, and partly on your own identity and experiences. A white American or European traveler, for example, will elicit very different reactions than a person of color. Tina Singleton discovered that she had not left racial prejudice behind in the United States when she spent one year in the Central African Republic as a child survival health specialist with the Peace Corps, then worked as the Peace Corps' first disability specialist in Cotonou, Benin. Singleton, who is hard of hearing, faced an unexpected obstacle as an African-American professional, because of the small number of minority development workers in the field. Some Beninese people, Singleton found, "considered it more desirable to work with a white colleague than a person of color—the status afforded many white people in the country was assumed to bring more benefits to the Beninese working alongside them. White volunteers were also considered to be more professionally competent." Singleton took this as a challenge, and worked to change the stereotypes. "I think this perspective began to change, slowly, as my Beninese colleagues and I worked together," she says. "We shared frank and often intense discussions about race, racism and the lingering effects of colonialism. And they respected my work."

Race played out differently for Don Galloway, a blind African-American man. "They were so delighted to have a brother with a disability come to their countries," he says. "I came with a different perspective from the typical middle-class white person with a disability." When he traveled in Africa and in the Caribbean, Galloway says he was treated like "a long-lost brother—almost like royalty!" He worked closely with the Southern African Federation of the Disabled. "When I left, they rolled out a red carpet. Literally! Someone called ahead to the airport, and they rolled out this red carpet up to the airplane!"

Gender is another variable that may affect your cultural experiences. "In many places, women who have disabilities are sort of non-people," says Jean Parker—though she hastens to add that she has encountered that combination of sexism and disability discrimination in her home country, the United States. When she travels, Parker says, "There's a tendency not to consult me for input on a decision, to talk about me in the third person."

One of the key cultural lessons shared by many international travelers is, simply, the importance of embracing opportunities to understand and respect different cultures. Zachary Battles, who is blind, volunteered to teach English to university students at the Language Institute in Kiev, Ukraine. "My short stay in Ukraine is one I will remember for life," says Battles. He says that he and the other volunteers on his team "faced the challenges of teaching with minimal experience and communicating with very little knowledge of either Russian or Ukrainian. However, armed with open minds and a desire to teach, we overcame these barriers and very much enjoyed our experiences." Essential to their success was their willingness "to experience as well as learn about a different culture," Battles says. "We enjoyed the cultural immersion afforded us by the hospitality of our host students. While living in the flats and homes of the students, we were introduced to many facets of the Ukrainian culture, such as cuisine, customs and language." From the these challenges and opportunities, Battles concludes, "Teachers must be willing to learn as well as teach."

Work, School and Home: Access and Accommodations in Different Exchange Settings

Whatever the purpose of your trip abroad, you will want to create the best possible conditions for success. The accommodations you use at work, school or home in your own country might be transferable. For example, a portable Braille writer can go with you, as can prescription medications, a raised toilet seat or a voice-controlled laptop computer. Even with these kinds of accommodations, you will need to consider the different environment in which you will be using the items. Research factors such as the electrical current differences and reliability, maintenance and repair options, and available medical resources.

You may also need to put in place new accommodations, similar to or different from accommodations you use in your home country. These should be appropriate both for your needs and for the local culture and conditions. Below you will find examples of accommodations that have worked for other disabled participants in international exchange programs.

Work and Internships

Putting your skills to work, and developing new skills, may require accommodations in your overseas workplace. Whether you are a volunteer, intern or a paid worker, you need to be able to fulfill your duties without disability-related obstacles.

Examples of workplace accommodations for people with various kinds of disabilities include:

- Teletypewriters (TTYs, for people that are deaf, hard of hearing or speech impaired)

- Sign language interpreters, especially for meetings, training sessions and other events where communication is important

- Telephone amplifiers for people with hearing impairments

- Braille labels for files, commonly used forms and office doorways

- Computers adapted with voice output, adapted keyboards or voice input

- Readers and scribes

- Tools adapted with cuffs or grips

- Accessible transportation to work assignments or relocation to an accessible office or workspace

- Job restructuring—for example, having co-workers take on the duties you are unable to perform, in exchange for you taking on some of their duties

- On-the-job assistance with learning routines, reading and writing, or handling personal assistance tasks

- Flexible work hours, workloads or deadlines

You may need to create some of your own accommodations, on the spot, as you discover what your job requires and what you are able to do. Approach your overseas work assignment with energy. Be open to trying new things. Don't let other people's expectations, or even your own doubts, limit the kinds of tasks you will take on. There will probably be some things you cannot do, but you may surprise yourself. Alan Shain has a physical disability, but he didn't shy away from physical labor when he worked with a group of Canadian youth during a building project in rural Costa Rica. He jumped into the job and figured out what he could and couldn't do. "I found I could do much of the light physical labor, such as clearing the land-site and laying down rocks for the floor," says Shain. In addition, he assumed responsibility for other jobs such as keeping track of the tools and managing finances. When his nondisabled colleagues saw Shain's willingness to do his share of the work, their respect for him increased.

Some disabled people, especially those participating in volunteer programs, may find themselves having to assert their ability to pull their own weight. Program administrators and co-workers may assume that demanding jobs, combined with the rigors of travel, are too much for people with physical or mental impairments. Frank Hernandez joined Up with People and toured Europe including Austria, Belgium, Denmark, Germany, Holland and Luxembourg. Because he is blind, he found that his supervisors did not assign him responsibilities equal to the other participants. "They didn't expect me to do any of the work that everybody else did," says Hernandez. They tried to spare him jobs such as setting up stage, sound and lighting equipment for the show. Hernandez insisted he wanted to work as hard as the other young participants, and to learn the same skills. First he approached his fellow participants who were already doing the full range of jobs. He asked questions, learned and volunteered to help do various tasks. Once he had proved himself to his peers, he approached the crew leader, then the cast manager, the show director, the tour director and finally the board of directors. Hernandez says it took him almost a month, and a great deal of persistence, to demonstrate that he could handle a full workload.

With the right access features and accommodations, combined with your own desire to dive in and get the job done, you can get the most out of your overseas work experience.

School

Arie Farnam studied in Germany for four months with the Educational Foundation. "School has posed the hardest problems related to my visual impairment," Farnam states. She found that getting text in large print has been very difficult, as has trying to take notes. Fortunately, Farnam brought along her own equipment. "Without my laptop computer," she says, "I would be lost."

Beth Ocrant, with a disability similar to Farnam's, had a much better experience during her study abroad program. During her junior year at Northern Illinois University (NIU), Ocrant studied at the University of Sunderland in England through the International Student Exchange Program. She planned ahead and found school officials on both sides of the Atlantic to be cooperative and helpful. "Well in advance," says Ocrant, "the disability services coordinator at Sunderland, the study abroad office at NIU, my vocational rehabilitation counselor and I formed a team. We figured out what I would need to have a successful experience and delegated who would take responsibility for each piece." She was able to arrange for accommodations such as audiotape versions of her textbooks, a computer with enlarging software and access to a closed-circuit television at the school library.

Ideally, you should be working closely with officials at both your home institution and your overseas school to arrange for the accommodations you will need. Other resources could be involved too, such as your vocational rehabilitation agency, your financial aid provider or disability organizations in the host country. Describe your needs fully and candidly discuss who will take responsibility for researching, obtaining and paying for your supports.

Supports in a school setting can include many of the same provisions described above for the workplace. In addition, educational activities may require accommodations such as:

- A notetaker in class and copies of overheads
- Permission to have extended time limits on tests
- A quiet study area free of distractions
- Tutoring
- Orientation to the campus
- Study materials in Braille, or on tape or disk
- Accessible transportation for field trips
- Counseling
- Real-time transcription or similar services

Sara Bianco, who is Deaf, participated in a six-month high school exchange to Germany through AFS Intercultural Programs. The program provided an American Sign Language interpreter for the pre-departure orientation, enabling Bianco to prepare alongside other participants. In Germany she attended a school for Deaf, hard-of-hearing and speech-impaired students. There she adapted, and then excelled. "I started out using gestures," Bianco says, "and left knowing four languages, including German Sign." Adaptations for Deaf participants at a foreign language school abroad for example, could include interactions using teletypewriters (TTYs) or computers to type dialogues between students in class, and one-on-one tutoring with a person who knows the local sign language.

Home

Finding suitable lodging should be part of your advance planning process, as described in Chapter 3, but housing issues may also arise while you are living abroad. Or you may find that your exchange program's typical housing arrangements won't work for you, due to inaccessibility, location or other factors. You may need to work with, or outside of, your exchange program to find the right living situation for you.

Donna Cencer, who has a mobility disability, traveled to Italy on a Rotary International Graduate Scholarship, and studied Italian literature at the University of Florence. It took her some time, and a willingness to try various situations, to find a good place to live. "During my first two weeks in Florence, I lived in two different hotels," she recalls. "Then I obtained housing in the only student dormitory in the city. However, this closet-sized room turned out to be unacceptable after one month. Then I found a centrally located room that included the use of a small kitchen." In trying to find suitable, accessible housing, Cencer relied on referrals from the people she met, which also led to an improvement in her communication skills. "In two months time, not only did I feel comfortable in my lodging and surroundings, but I also felt content with my increasing Italian vocabulary and language skills." Cencer attributes her eventual success to her resourcefulness and adaptability. "By the end of my experience," she says, "I felt that Italy had made me as flexible as mozzarella cheese."

Your home away from home could be more than just a place to eat, sleep and study. Your living situation may also provide you with relationships and resources. Paddy Collins-Bohrer, a student at the School Without Walls in Rochester, New York, participated in an exchange program in Novgorod, Russia. His homestay situation played an important role in making his Russian experience rich and successful. "I was placed with a wonderful family who had been briefed on what type of help I needed," says Collins-Bohrer, who has a mobility impairment. "They lived on the third floor in an apartment with a working elevator, so I never had to climb the stairs. Also, my family owned a car in which, on some days, my exchange sister and I were driven to our activities. But there were some days when the car was not available and we either had to take a taxi or the bus. I quickly discovered the taxi was much easier for me to take, but my friends were always ready and willing to help me take the bus."

Families with members with disabilities may be an alternative advantage. Sara Bianco found her housing placement to be supportive and accessible. She was placed with Deaf parents and hearing brothers, all of whom helped her to learn German Sign Language. "My homestay family was great," says Bianco. Similarly, Marie Sharp, a wheelchair user who studied abroad at the University of São Paulo, Brazil, lived with a woman who also uses a wheelchair. "It was very easy to get around her house," says

Sharp. "More important, my host mother and I became very good friends. She was instrumental in helping me adapt to life in Brazil. I admire and respect her so much. She's a beautiful person with a strong and powerful spirit that motivated me many times."

Frank Hernandez had both positive and negative experiences with his living arrangements during the Up with People tour. "Some host families in Europe wanted to baby me," says Hernandez, who is blind. His longest stay was in Germany, where he spent four weeks. He stayed with a single mother and her teenage son. They didn't always understand or agree with each other, but the host mother was very upfront with him and listened to his perspectives. For example, he wanted to use his limited transportation budget to rent a tandem bicycle to ride with one of his partners. The host mother was worried about this, and wanted to give him money for taxis instead. He did not feel that would be fair, and refused. By the time he left Germany, Hernandez and his host mother had learned to like and respect each other.

Most frequently, cultural insights flow from the personal relationships between travelers and their new friends and acquaintances. For example, Rhonda Neuhaus, who wears two below-knee prostheses, spent five months in Costa Rica learning about environmental problems and solutions as a participant in the School for Field Studies. During the weekends, all participants were assigned to live with host families. "I found this to be a great experience," Neuhaus says. She spoke candidly about her disability, and in return her host family treated her with respect, admiration and affection. "I truly became a part of their family," Neuhaus recalls fondly. "Together we attended local fairs, hiked in the nearby mountains, and cooked Costa Rican specialties. I am honored to have had the opportunity to be a part of their lives and to have been welcomed with the love, generosity and warmth they constantly extended towards me." As a result of these and other experiences, Neuhaus enjoyed incalculable gains in her self-confidence and awareness of the world and its people. "I explored a new country and its environmental issues, improved my Spanish language skills, made new friends and realized that anything is possible," she says. Neuhaus returned later to see this family again and work in marketing for a yoga center in Costa Rica.

Homestay situations offer many opportunities for learning different cultural norms, and building friendships across those cultural differences. Leticia Arellano, a Mexican-American Deaf woman, lived with a Japanese family, teaching them American Sign Language in exchange for room and board. At one point, Arellano told her host mother that she missed hugs. "Deaf Americans tend to hug every time we meet. Deaf Japanese just bow and show their greetings." Arellano was delighted with her host mother's response: "Nariko was surprised, and she told me she would be more than happy to give me some hugs."

For a person whose disability may cause fatigue, host families that offer

Be aware of how much your own values and your definition of concepts such as "independence" and "access" color your perception of what is happening around you. Be open to new ways of seeing and thinking.

assistance with laundry or cooking may be a blessing. Such a situation may free you from having to do daily chores that can tax your energy, and leave you more energy for things like further exploring the local surroundings and host culture. Finding the right living situation, and working out any kinks in that situation, will be well worth the effort. Many exchange participants with disabilities report that their overseas home away from home was the most memorable and rewarding aspect of their trip. The right homestay placement can provide accessibility, support and lifelong connections.

Chapter Five

Coming Home

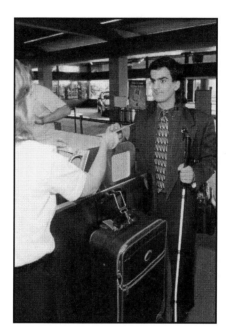

When your journey is over, it may take you some time to understand how your travels have changed you, and to integrate those changes into your life. After you arrive home, gently allow yourself the time to rest and reflect, and even more time go through the reverse culture shock that may effect returning travelers. This was the experience of Shanda Grubb, who has cerebral palsy, when she returned to the United States from Russia after serving as a volunteer with Wheels for the World. "I needed time to readjust to the American way of life," she recalls. "My body and mind craved space to recover and process all that had happened, not to mention overcoming jet lag!"

Will it all be worth it? After you've envisioned, chosen, planned and finally made your trip, how will your life be different? How will you integrate your international experiences into the rest of your life?

If other travelers' experiences are any indication, chances are you will learn important lessons, both large and small, that will help you map your future course—your personal interests and career goals—based partly on the new perspectives you gain.

Forging Bonds Across Cultures: Alliances and Friendships

Some of the strongest, most treasured memories shared by these disabled travelers revolve around relationships with people they met while working or studying abroad. Marta Lukjan, who as an undergraduate studied for nine months at the University of Queensland in Australia, fondly recalls the friends she made at the Women's College where she lived. "Nine years later I still get invitations to their weddings!" Lukjan says. Such lifelong connections have enriched Lukjan's life, and so has the inspiration she took from these strong young women, whom Lukjan describes as "extraordinary young people with a knack for growing. They taught me about strength, about knowing when you are equal to others and proving it." These students became Lukjan's role models and dear friends. "I learned through living in Women's College what a support network can do," she says.

Solidarity seems to be a common theme for travelers abroad, especially those who participate in exchange programs that focus on social change issues. Many people gain a new appreciation of their place in the global community, their connections to people throughout the world and their obligations to their fellow human beings. This awareness may come about through education about social issues, or through personal connections—or both. Jessica Aaron, who uses a wheelchair, has traveled to Latin America several times during college and graduate school. "As my awareness of cultural and disability issues grew, so did my understanding of myself and of disability matters in the United States. I learned that people with disabilities all over the world share common challenges. [Working together] we make widespread, lasting changes."

Relationships and conversations are a rich source of education for travelers abroad. When people come together around common interests and issues, lively discussions emerge. These discussions may last for an hour or for decades. In either case, they can deepen and broaden a traveler's worldview or problem-solving strategies, suggest new career choices, shape ideas and convictions, and encourage action upon return.

Exchange participants' connections with their counterparts in other countries can become a powerful motivating force and opportunity for expanding knowledge. Gerardo Nigenda, a former intern at a non-profit agency in the United States who is blind, has participated in several international exchanges. He says the lengthy, lively discussions he's enjoyed with Palestinians, Danes, Japanese, Slovaks and others "have enriched my life and my work with ideas, thoughts, ways of confronting problems, and expanded my knowledge. Each of these experiences has renewed my confidence in the power of people to come together to resolve problems and remove physical, political, attitudinal and economic barriers."

Just as you enjoyed contacts with other travelers while you were abroad, upon your return you will find other people who have returned from overseas and want to keep on sharing experiences. Don't put your experiences on a shelf and forget about them. You can keep expanding your circle of friends with international interests. You will find new connections with people simply because you share a common experience of being an international traveler.

For Rachael Abbott, a young visually impaired woman who traveled to Costa Rica, personal connections became the focus of her activities during her trip, and from this she gained important self-knowledge. "One thing I've learned is that everybody has different interests and talents," says Abbott. "There were people on my trip who were really good at knowing legislative issues and knowing how to make things better." In contrast, Abbott found that she was much more in tune with individuals' personal feelings and experiences. "When I was in Costa Rica, I learned about disability rights and disability access," she recalls, "but at the same time, I was concerned with their personal lives. I was concerned with their everyday issues, their friendships, things like that, and how they struggle with their disability." This realization led Abbott to major in psychology in college, and she intends to make a career of counseling disabled people, helping them with personal adjustment and other issues. "I want to get my Master's degree in family therapy," she says, "because I realize there are not a lot of specialists in disability."

Some disabled travelers gain a new sense of themselves and their place in their community, in their culture, or even in their family. Sharon Nguyen, who has cerebral palsy, had always wanted to visit Vietnam, where her parents and grandparents came from. Having grown up in the United States, she also wanted to make cross-cultural connections around the subject of disability. She began forging bonds both with people working for disability organizations and with relatives from both sides of her family. "People in Vietnam greeted me with open arms," Nguyen says, "often coming up to talk to me as if we knew each other. I hope to visit my homeland again to help improve accessibility and build leadership for people with disabilities."

Revelations on the Road: Travelers Gain Self-knowledge

Rachel Abbott's experience in Costa Rica—her discovery of her own talents and her resulting career choice—is but one example of travelers learning about themselves by traveling to another country. Perhaps the dramatic change of venue, the removal from one's accustomed context, allows a new light to shine into places usually shaded by habit or complacency. Traveling overseas, as we've seen throughout this book, forces a person to view things from a different perspective, adapt to situations and perhaps solve problems that would likely never arise in his or her hometown. Succeeding in gaining new perspectives and meeting challenges can bring out strengths and skills you never imagined you had.

Even when you fall short of meeting the challenges of travel, you may learn about yourself, and find yourself testing out and developing new perceptions, abilities and coping strategies. During an earlier trip abroad as a teenager, Abbott felt insecure about herself and her visual impairment and therefore had not learned to ask for what she needed. On that exchange to Chile, Abbott had been excited to go but says, "When I was there, I kind of felt left out." She avoided some group activities such as hiking, because she was too embarrassed to ask for help. "I didn't want to ask, 'Hey, do you mind walking with me when we go hiking, so I don't trip over a rock or something?' I was around all these teenagers in a new setting and not able to speak the language," says Abbott. "It made me face my disability." She reflects, "It taught me not to be so shy, to work on being more confident and outgoing."

Later, as a college student, she traveled to Israel with a school group. This time, she took a different approach. "I was more assertive. I wanted to make sure I had somebody to stay with me, so I could always find the group. In Israel, the streets are crowded

157

with people, and it's very easy to get separated from a group." By asking for help, Abbott developed a clearer sense of herself and her disability-related needs.

Many other disabled travelers report similar increases in their ability to manage different aspects of their disabilities as a result of going overseas. Unfamiliar situations and logistical challenges call for new coping skills, innovative techniques and more decisive action on the part of the traveler abroad. Such opportunities for personal growth are valuable for anyone, but particularly for people with disabilities. "I learned to be more resourceful and more flexible in various situations," says Jean Lin, who has cerebral palsy, "and to be more aware of my surroundings and to be more adaptable to the environment."

International travel can also build confidence. Alona Brown spent a semester studying in Alicante, Spain. As a result of her experience, Brown says that her self-esteem "went up 100 percent." "Here I was a blind individual, I didn't know the language that well, I'm older and I'm African-American. I didn't know many of the challenges I would be faced with and I didn't know if I would be accepted," recalls Brown. "I did it," she adds. "I met every challenge, and I was warmly received. Now I have bigger dreams for myself, and the courage to pursue them."

Overseas travel may put your typical experiences in a broader perspective. Shanda Grubb, who has cerebral palsy, traveled to Russia as a volunteer with Wheels for the World, a nonprofit organization which distributes wheelchairs and other equipment in various countries. "The experience in Russia continues to affect my life even now—often as a reference point in daily life," Grubb says. "As everyday challenges pop up, related to my disability or not, I often think, 'If I adapted to Russia, I can here too!' As I look back at the experiences, I'm thankful for the hard times and the good ones. Every moment taught me something new about who I am and the kind of person I want to be."

You may also discover new interests—particular social issues, a certain cuisine, a language, the history of a country, an art form such as flamenco dance or Renaissance sculpture. The rewards of international friendships may become your new passion. Jean Marchant says her participation in a foreign exchange program "definitely made me want to be a homestay provider, and as a consequence I have met people with disabilities who stayed at my house from all over the world."

A More Complex and Exciting World: Travelers Learn Cultural Lessons

Among the effects of international travel on disabled and nondisabled individuals alike, cultural awareness is often the most marked change. This may include an enlarged view of the many possibilities in the world. Says Frank Hernandez: "International travel offers people with disabilities the opportunity to see different ways of doing things," such as communicating, getting around and functioning when access is less than perfect.

David Dye, a graduate student in international relations who has a significant hearing loss, participated in two different study programs in Brazil—one in Rio de Janeiro and one in São Paulo— where he learned Portuguese and studied economic and business conditions. He found he was very compatible with Brazilian society, and he experienced great joy in meeting many warm and friendly people there. "Brazilians are, without a doubt, some of the most generous, fun people on the planet," Dye says. "As a matter of fact, I've felt depressed and a bit lost since my return to the United States." However, he knew he would return to what he had come to think of as his new home.

Many travelers become so comfortable with the values and lifestyle of their host country that they experience a kind of reverse culture shock when they return home. For example, Pamela Houston, who has cerebral palsy, spent time in Peru, and despite initial difficulties, she eventually came to feel very much at home there. She says: "Coming back to the States was like... well, coming to a foreign country. Everything looked so different, so extravagant, overdone and pompous.... my eyes and heart had adjusted so thoroughly to Peru."

During her trip to Costa Rica, Daisy Sipp met people who were Deaf, like her, but who lacked the educational advantages that she enjoyed. She saw Deaf adults learning basic literacy and elementary math, because they had not received schooling when they were young. "After leaving Costa Rica, I felt that it was part of my duty to help educate Deaf children in other countries."

Many disabled travelers return home with convictions about advocating for social justice issues, after witnessing what they perceive to be injustices abroad. These may take different forms in different places, but there are common threads that extend worldwide. It may be harder to recognize injustice in your own backyard; it's so familiar that it seems normal. Perhaps this is why many international travelers seem to recall examples of oppression overseas—why injustice seems more obvious in a foreign context. Some of the most vivid cultural lessons brought home by disabled travelers are those involving human rights advocacy. Many people return with a strong sense of global solidarity, and a greater desire to fight for what's right. "It's so easy in the U.S. to become cocooned," says Jean Marchant, who has multiple sclerosis. In the small German town of Oberwasel, she saw disabled people who were segregated and shunned, and others who were actively organizing for change. "It made me a stronger advocate for people with disabilities and their rights, internationally as well as nationally. Now, when I see something, I don't just stay quiet and say, 'That's terrible.' I speak up! I've become good at writing letters and all the stuff that one needs to do to be a voice of activism and a squeaky wheel, because I had first-hand experience with how life can be for people with disabilities in countries outside of the United States."

Another important outcome of international travel is the opportunity to learn techniques and skills that can encourage both individuals and communities to work for increased opportunities. People on exchanges can learn new strategies from each other, a benefit that reaches across all interests, academic disciplines and professions. Both sides of an exchange benefit from shared learning. Tia Nelis, a leader in the self-advocacy movement

You may have taken a language class before you went abroad, which helped introduce you to your host country's people and culture. Now that you are home, don't let those valuable language skills you've practiced overseas go to waste. Take up a language class or start a weekly conversational group in your area to maintain and improve your language skills.

in the United States, credits an international exchange with fueling her initial local organizing efforts. Years ago, representatives of People First of Canada came to Illinois to meet with people with developmental disabilities. That contact got Nelis and others interested in starting a People First group of their own. Recently, Nelis traveled to Belgium to meet with people with developmental disabilities whose self-advocacy movement is still new. As people continue to cross borders, they pass on the motivation and the strategies to change their societies.

Travelers who go abroad to offer their skills—as volunteers, visiting speakers or consultants—almost always find that they learn as much as they teach. When Nelis went to Belgium to share her knowledge and experience concerning self-advocacy, she found that Belgian counterparts were addressing this topic in an innovative way. The government was planning to publish an informational booklet about disability resources, and the local self-advocates were reviewing it for readability. The group found that most people with developmental disabilities would be unable to comprehend the book, which used long words and complicated sentences. "They took a highlighter," says Nelis, "and they highlighted all the stuff that they didn't understand, then gave it back and said, 'Put it in simpler language.'" Nelis brought this idea back home to her People First group, which later implemented the same strategy to make policy documents and other written materials more accessible to people with cognitive disabilities.

Many other travelers reported being changed forever by seeing different cultural attitudes toward disabled people—and also by meeting people dedicated to changing the cultural status quo. David Oaks vividly recalls visiting one of the poorest neighborhoods in Santiago, Chile. "We visited one of the few places there for people who were diagnosed with psychiatric disabilities," says

Oaks. When he found he was getting VIP treatment that separated him from the clients, he encouraged the hosts to seat the visitors with the clients during snack time. This fostered inclusion, rather than a separation that was not comfortable for Oaks and isolating for clients.

Another trip abroad offered Oaks an example of leadership in action. During a trip to Oslo, Norway, he visited Arnold Juklerod, a person working for the rights of people diagnosed with psychiatric disabilities. Juklerod drew attention to the issue of institutionalization by doing a long-term sit-in in the recreation building of a local psychiatric facility. Oaks says," I felt humbled by meeting him and other people. They had been working for years on this major campaign, hundreds of people." Not only was he impressed with their level of organization and work, but the experience gave Oaks a renewed commitment as he returned home.

Increased cultural awareness often leads to personal growth for international travelers. Leticia Arellano, an American who is Deaf, lived in Japan for ten weeks, teaching American Sign Language and learning Japanese Sign Language and Japanese Deaf culture. "Sharing the cultures, values and sign languages increased my understanding of other Deaf, and hearing, people all over the world," Arellano says.

Telling the Story: Share Your Experiences with Others

After you return from working, studying or volunteering abroad, you'll bring with you a valuable commodity—the story of your trip. While you're settling back into your home environment, you will want to think about how to share your story with others.

Many travelers have found great satisfaction in recounting their adventures, describing their experiences overseas and articulating their conclusions.

There are many different ways you can share your story. You can:

- Write a guest column for your local or campus newspaper's opinion page or feature section.

- Write an article for a specialty magazine focusing on the type of subjects, issues or work you engaged in during your trip.

- Make presentations for community groups, international associations, college or high school classes, youth groups, service clubs or advocacy organizations. Your presentations may take several forms, including:

  o A slide show with narration and recorded music

  o A reading from your travel journals

  o A formal report on your study project, with maps, charts, graphs, photos or other illustrations

  o A demonstration of a skill you learned

  o A talk describing your trip, followed by a question-and-answer period.

- Write an academic paper or a discussion paper, and present it at a relevant conference.

- Create a web site where you can post photos, journal entries, interviews and even audio and video files.

Sharing the story with others offers numerous benefits. You may earn college credit or have your report published. Depending on the extent of your international experience, you could gain recognition as a specialist in your field or in the particular region that you visited. You may also fulfill obligations to groups who sponsored your travel.

As you share stories with other travelers, you may also become inspired to explore other destinations, or you will motivate others to become involved in an exchange program themselves. Wendy Harbour, a Deaf professional, first traveled abroad as a high school student to Japan, but has since ventured to places such as Malaysia, Singapore and Venezuela. In addition, her positive experience in Japan started her whole family's interest in traveling abroad and in hosting international students in their home.

Most rewarding of all in sharing your experiences, you may find yourself reliving your travels and understanding them even more deeply, by virtue of having to reflect upon your time abroad while preparing your presentation, article, paper or website. Thus you can bring your newfound knowledge and wisdom home for keeps, making it part of your life and your community.

Values and Skills: The Impact of International Exchange on Travelers' Lives and Work

Exchange participants with disabilities often bring home more than friendships, memories and enlarged perspectives. Many come back ready to take on new roles in their communities and careers. These new roles may include any of the following:

- Serve as a peer advisor, volunteer or advisory committee member for an exchange organization you participated with or that is located in your hometown.

- Explore other international exchange trips to deepen or diversify your knowledge or host exchange participants coming to your country.

- Find an internship or volunteer with an international visitors program in your area.

- Consider an international career or bring international perspectives to your current one.

- Revise academic course content and develop new course work at your local school, college, university or continuing education program.

- Develop other exchange programs, for example a professional exchange program between your home and host communities.

- Form an informal alumni group on campus or in your community, or join a formal alumni association serving your group.

Many disabled travelers find great value in the very things that make their host country so different from their home country. For example, some visitors to the United States express admiration for the accessible facilities, assistive technology and nondiscrimination laws, all of which may translate to expanded opportunities available to disabled people. "I was able to bring back information on [accessible] buses to my country," says one past participant in an exchange program sponsored by MIUSA. "In fact, because of that, now we have an almost accessible bus system."

Returning exchange participants also possess confidence and abilities, gained from responding to challenging situations, navigating different cultures and environments, and adapting to major changes—all part of the international travel experience. Adaptability and self-knowledge are preferred qualifications for many occupations. A good example is Jessica Voigts, who, during her sophomore year in college, interned for an international exchange foundation in Tokyo. Voigts has a mobility impairment, and had to learn to get along without her usual support systems and modes of transportation. She endured inconvenience and hardship at first, but she learned new ways of doing things, and found understanding and support from people she met there. "In Japan I had become aware of my disability in a way that I was unlikely to have gained in the United States," Voigts summarizes. "In an environment that presented barriers, my disability was something that I could creatively and flexibly deal with in almost any situation." Such creativity and flexibility became definite assets in Voigts' future employment. "This has served me well in all aspects of my life," she says, "and prepared me for a later job in London as a resident director for summer study abroad programs."

Furthermore, solid skills make these returned travelers more attractive to prospective employers, and make them more effective in a variety of occupations. In one survey of former exchange participants, many affirmed that their international exchange experience had brought them concrete benefits in terms of their employability, job competence and leadership capacity. One person applied for a job as a camp program director, supervising a multi-national staff. The employer was favorably impressed by the time spent overseas. "It did spark questions in my job interview," she said. "I'm sure that my international experience really helped me to get the job."

International contacts are another vital outcome for exchange participants who are disabled. One traveler gained a worldwide community that became a support system and a valuable consulting resource. "When I have problems in my work," this participant remarked, "I email friends that were on my exchange, or give them a call or write them a letter and they say, 'I've dealt with that.'"

Heather Harker, who is Deaf, has traveled and worked in Russia, Malaysia, Thailand and several other countries. Each of these experiences gave Harker new perspectives and new opportunities to develop her talents and expertise. Now she works as a nonprofit consultant in New England. Harker's view of leadership, and the techniques she uses to promote leadership opportunities, evolved considerably as a result of her experiences abroad as a Fellow with the Kellogg International Leadership Program. "When people are committed to common goals, work together to accomplish them and ensure continuity by passing on leadership to others, they will experience positive change in their community. Prior to my work experiences in Malaysia," says Harker, "I felt that change was all about institutions, policies and government. Now, I understand that change is about ourselves and the people around us—whether we are in government, the nonprofit sector, our families, or even at a neighborhood barbecue."

Every person with a disability who participates in an international exchange experience will make an impact on the world, and will be affected in return, Harker believes. "There is good work that needs to be done everywhere in the world," she says. "A disabled student in an international exchange program can make a difference simply by educating nondisabled colleagues that it is possible for a person with a disability to participate. A volunteer in an international work-camp makes a difference in the lives of those who are affected by her/his work. A policy maker advocating accessible telecommunications is making a difference. Life is a journey and our goal should be to enjoy it, but also to give something back to those who follow after us."

Travel abroad can be a tremendously enriching and fulfilling life experience, not only for you, but for those you come in contact with too. The impact of your experience abroad will increase after you return, as you share stories with others, maintain the friendships you developed abroad and incorporate your newfound cross-cultural skills and perspectives in your life and future work. Prepare to come back a changed person—with enhanced career opportunities, maybe some new language skills, cross-cultural friendships, new self-discoveries, and a broader view of the world and the opportunities that lay before you.

Now that you've learned so much and met so many interesting people from overseas, what can you do to build on these foundations? Some people return from an exchange and work with local universities or other venues to host musical groups they heard overseas, thus introducing their home community to people and sounds they encountered abroad. Another traveler, after meeting craftswomen who make baskets, came home and set up a cooperative export business to give the profits directly back to the women. Other travelers have started nonprofit agencies, developed new exchange programs, written books, and much more. What will you do?

Appendix A:
National Clearinghouse on Disability and Exchange

The National Clearinghouse on Disability and Exchange (NCDE), a project sponsored by the Bureau of Educational and Cultural Affairs of the United States Department of State and administered by Mobility International USA (MIUSA), provides free information and referral to individuals with disabilities interested in participating in international study, work, volunteer or research programs overseas. NCDE also advises exchange programs and colleges and universities on how to accommodate participants with disabilities in their exchange programs. Visit the NCDE website to search its online exchange program database or to find information on NCDE's publications, peer network and services. Contact NCDE if you have any questions related to people with disabilities pursuing international exchange opportunities:

NATIONAL CLEARINGHOUSE ON DISABILITY AND EXCHANGE
Mobility International USA
PO Box 10767
Eugene, OR 97440 USA
Tel/TTY: (541) 343-1284
Fax: (541) 343-6812
E-mail: clearinghouse@miusa.org
Web: www.miusa.org

NCDE Information Sheets

The following is a list of information sheets on frequently requested topics that NCDE has produced. Some of these information sheets can be found online at www.miusa.org/publications, or contact NCDE to obtain copies and alternative formats.

Resources on International Exchange Programs:

1. Disability Studies programs
2. Disability-related exchange opportunities
3. English language programs in the United States
4. General exchange resources
5. High school exchanges
6. Homestay exchanges
7. International service opportunities
8. Interning abroad
9. Professional exchanges
10. Senior exchanges
11. Short-term work exchange programs
12. Teacher exchanges and teaching abroad programs

Other Information Sheets:

1. Air travel for people with disabilities
2. Americans with Disabilities Act information and resources
3. Arranging for personal assistants abroad
4. ASL videos, classes and books
5. Financial aid for individuals with disabilities interested in exchange
6. Information on the use of Supplemental Security Income and vocational rehabilitation funding for exchange
7. Reasonable accommodation information for many types of disabilities

8. Traveling with a service dog
9. Traveling with medications
10. Universal design resources
11. Visa resources
12. Women with disabilities organizations

NCDE Customized Referral Services

In addition to the information sheets and online databases mentioned above, NCDE offers customized information and referral services focused on an individual's specific disability, exchange program preferences or countries of interest. If you have access to the internet, explore NCDE's website resources to begin your search, then contact NCDE or fill out our online form to request individualized information.

NCDE Roundtable Consortium

NCDE's advisory committee, the Roundtable Consortium, is a collaborative effort among Mobility International USA (MIUSA), the U.S. Department of State's Bureau of Educational and Cultural Affairs and 24 international exchange and disability-related organizations. The Roundtable Consortium advises NCDE on strategies to design programs, products and services that promote the inclusion of people with disabilities in international exchange. Roundtable members then help implement those efforts within their own organizations and beyond, as leaders in the disability and international exchange fields. Below, you will find an organizational description of each member along with the organization's website.

MIUSA's National Clearinghouse on Disability and Exchange works to increase the participation of people with disabilities in all types of international exchange programs. www.miusa.org/ncde

The U.S. Department of State's Bureau of Educational and Cultural Affairs, which sponsors NCDE, promotes mutual understanding between U.S. citizens and people from 150 countries worldwide through a diverse range of academic, professional and cultural exchange programs and activities. http://exchanges.state.gov

AFS Intercultural Programs promotes intercultural awareness among families, youth and educators around the world. AFS offers several program options including high school, college and secondary school teacher programs in 55 countries. www.afs.org

Alliance for International Educational and Cultural Exchange is an association of 68 nonprofit organizations comprising the international educational and cultural exchange community in the United States. Its mission is to formulate and promote public policies that support international exchange programs. www.alliance-exchange.org

American Association of People with Disabilities is a non-profit, cross-disability membership organization advocating for the rights of disabled Americans. Its goals further the productivity, independence, full citizenship and total integration of people with disabilities into all aspects of society and the natural environment. www.aapd-dc.org

Association on Higher Education and Disability is an international, multi-cultural organization of professionals committed to full participation in higher education for people with disabilities. The association promotes excellence through education, communication, training and conferences. www.ahead.org

Center for International Rehabilitation Research Information and Exchange has the mission to increase access to information and experts on rehabilitation research worldwide, thereby improving the practice of rehabilitation in the United States and abroad. http://cirrie.buffalo.edu

Council on International Educational Exchange is a nonprofit, nongovernmental organization dedicated to helping people gain understanding, acquire knowledge and develop skills for living in a globally interdependent and culturally diverse world. It develops and administers many exchange programs throughout the world for high school and college students as well as for professionals. **www.ciee.org**

Council on Standards for International Educational Travel is a nonprofit organization committed to quality international youth exchange. It establishes standards for high school foreign exchange organizations and annually publishes the *Advisory List of International Educational Travel and Exchange Programs*. **www.csiet.org**

Disabled Peoples' International aims to extend the principles of human rights to all people with disabilities, including the right to full participation in their families, their communities, their nations and in all spheres of their lives. It works to keep individuals and disability-related organizations informed about disability issues around the world and also to foster community building and support. **www.dpi.org**

Disability Rights Education and Defense Fund is a nonprofit disability law and policy center run primarily by people with disabilities and parents of children with disabilities. It has forged alliances with disability organizations around the world and has consulted on disability policy and programs in 17 countries. **www.dredf.org**

George Washington University HEATH Resource Center is the national clearinghouse for information about education after high school for people with disabilities. It provides written materials on a variety of topics related to post-secondary education for students with disabilities. www.heath.gwu.edu

Institute of International Education is committed to strengthening international understanding and cooperation through international study, research and practical training programs. It produces numerous exchange-related publications and administers a number of programs, including the Fulbright and other grant programs. www.iie.org or www.iiepassport.org

International Volunteer Programs Association is an alliance of nonprofit, non-governmental organizations based in the Americas that are involved in international volunteer and internship exchanges. This organization encourages excellence and responsibility in the field of international voluntarism and promotes public awareness of and greater access to international volunteer programs. www.volunteerinternational.org

NAFSA: Association of International Educators is an organization whose 9,000 members include foreign student advisors, study abroad advisors, international admissions officers, teachers and administrators of English as a Second Language programs and community volunteers involved in international educational exchange. Members come from all 50 states and 60 countries. www.nafsa.org

National Council for International Visitors is a network of community and national nongovernmental organizations and institutions, the mission of which is to improve international relations through professional and personal communication and exchange.

Local councils regularly arrange for international visitors to meet and share ideas with leaders in both the private and public sector. **www.nciv.org**

National Youth Leadership Network is a youth-driven, youth-led organization comprised of young adult leaders with disabilities. The network strives to promote leadership development and education ensuring that all youth with disabilities have the opportunity to attain their maximum, unique and personal potential. **www.nyln.org**

Paralyzed Veterans of America administers programs in advocacy, sports and recreation, spinal cord injury treatment research, legislative lobbying, transportation, employment and disability rights. **www.pva.org**

Partners of the Americas is a private, voluntary inter-American organization that works to improve the quality of life in the Americas and the Caribbean. Sixty partnerships link 45 U.S. states with 31 countries in Latin America and the Caribbean for technical assistance and cultural exchange activities in the fields of agriculture, community education, rehabilitation, preventative health programs, the arts, disaster relief and women in development. **www.partners.net**

Rotary Foundation supports the efforts of Rotary International, an international organization engaged in a variety of youth, professional and educator exchanges. Rotary works toward world understanding and peace through local, national and international humanitarian, educational and cultural programs. **www.rotary.org**

Sister Cities International is committed to the goal of strengthening global understanding by encouraging and assisting sister city relationships between U.S. communities and cities throughout the world. The goal for the cities involved is to learn more about each other and to develop lasting and meaningful exchanges of citizens. www.sister-cities.org

Technical Assistance Alliance for Parent Centers is a project that supports a unified technical assistance system under the Individuals with Disabilities Education Act. This project is funded by the U.S. Department of Education, Office of Special Education Programs and offers varied resources for families of children and young adults with disabilities. The Technical Assistance Alliance is one of 28 projects located at PACER Center in Minnesota. www.taalliance.org or www.pacer.org

University of New Orleans Training, Resource and Assistive-Technology Center promotes international exchange opportunities for students with disabilities. It also provides technology-intensive training and resources for individuals with disabilities in order to promote independence and increased employability. www.uno.edu/~trac

World Institute on Disability is a nonprofit, international public-policy center dedicated to carrying out cutting edge research on disability issues and overcoming obstacles to independent living. Its International Division serves as a center for the international exchange of information and expertise on disability and disability policy. www.wid.org

Youth For Understanding is dedicated to intercultural understanding and world peace through exchange programs for high school students. The organization currently operates exchange programs in nearly 50 countries in Africa, Asia, Europe, North America, South America and the Pacific. www.youthforunderstanding.org

Appendix B: Resources

International Exchange Opportunities

The following are those exchange-related opportunities mentioned throughout *Survival Strategies*; this is only a partial listing of the many exchange programs and funding sources available. Each exchange organization's level of experience accommodating people with disabilities in its programs will vary. NCDE staff are ready to assist you, the exchange organizations and educational institutions by answering follow-up questions and providing suggestions to ensure a successful international experience. For more opportunities, search the publications and websites listed below.

ACDI/VOCA
50 F Street NW, Suite 1075
Washington, DC 20001 USA
Tel: (202) 383-4961
Fax: (202) 783-7204
E-mail: webmaster@acdivoca.org
Web: www.acdivoca.org

ACDI/VOCA is a private, non-profit international development organization providing technical expertise at the request of farmers, agribusinesses, cooperatives, and private and government agencies abroad. With a base of skilled volunteers, ACDI/VOCA helps develop economic opportunities for farmers and others all over the world. Opportunities are primarily for U.S. residents to participate as volunteers abroad.

AMERICAN ASSOCIATION OF UNIVERSITY WOMEN
AAUW Educational Foundation
1111 Sixteenth Street NW
Washington, DC 20036 USA
Tel: (800) 326-2289
Fax: (202) 785-7777
E-mail: info@aauw.org
Web: www.aauw.org

The AAUW Educational Foundation provides funding for graduate women worldwide and supports aspiring scholars around the globe, teachers and activists in local communities, women at important stages of their careers and those pursuing professions where women are underrepresented. The foundation funds research; fellowships and grants for outstanding women from around the globe; special awards; community action projects; and symposia, roundtables, and forums.

CANADIAN CROSSROADS INTERNATIONAL
317 Adelaide Street West, Suite 500
Toronto, Ontario M5V 1P9 CANADA
Tel: (416) 967-1611
Fax: (416) 967-9078
E-mail: info@cciorg.ca
Web: www.cciorg.ca

Canadian Crossroads International provides overseas programs to groups going to Francophone African countries for eight weeks or to individuals desiring a 14-week community placement volunteering in developing countries and living with host families.

CENTER FOR GLOBAL EDUCATION
Augsburg College
2211 Riverside Avenue
Minneapolis, MN 55454 USA
Tel: (800) 299-8889 or (612) 330-1159
Fax: (612) 330-1695
E-mail: globaled@augsburg.edu
Web: www.augsburg.edu/global

Augsburg College's Center for Global Education (CGE) offers semester abroad programs featuring local lecturers and homestay living arrangements. CGE's short-term travel seminars run for one to three weeks during which participants are introduced to local people and learn about their issues, challenges and culture. The customized educational travel program includes faculty development seminars for educators, short-term programs for college and university students, and enhancements to travel or study programs already in place.

COUNCIL ON INTERNATIONAL EDUCATIONAL EXCHANGE
7 Custom House Street, 3rd Floor
Portland, ME 04101 USA
Tel: (800) 407-8839
Fax: (207) 553-7699
E-mail: studyinfo@ciee.org
Web: www.ciee.org

The Council on International Educational Exchange develops and administers educational exchange programs throughout the world for high school and college students as well as for professionals. The organization also administers an international voluntary service program and a work-abroad program for college students.

FORD FOUNDATION
Grants and Fellowships for Organizations and Individuals
320 West 43rd Street
New York, NY 10017 USA
Tel: (212) 573-5000
Fax: (212) 351-3677
E-mail: office-secretary@fordfound.org
Web: www.fordfound.org

The Ford Foundation accepts proposals for funding in the following areas of interest: urban poverty, rural poverty, social justice, governance, public policy, education, culture, international affairs, reproductive health and population. Most of the Foundation's grant funds are given to organizations. Individual grants and graduate-level scholarships are limited to research, training and other activities related to its program interests.

FREEMAN AWARDS FOR STUDY IN ASIA
Institute of International Education
809 United Nations Plaza
New York, NY 10017 USA
Tel: (212) 984-5542
E-mail: Freeman-ASIA@iie.org
Web: www.iie.org/programs/freeman-asia

The Institute of International Education (IIE) administers the Freeman Awards for Study in Asia sponsored by the Freeman Foundation. Designed to promote undergraduate academic study in Asia, this award provides funding in amounts from $3000-$7000, depending on the length of the program. It can be used for study in one of fifteen Asian countries. The award is available to students with demonstrated financial need and priority will be given to students with no previous experience in the country where they plan to study.

LIONS CLUBS INTERNATIONAL
300 West 22nd Street
Oak Brook, IL 60521 USA
Tel: (630) 571-5466
Fax: (630) 571-8890
E-mail: lions@lionsclubs.org
Web: www.lionsclubs.org

Lions Clubs International is a worldwide community service organization. It awards financial assistance such as scholarships and also provides funds for purchasing equipment.

MARSHALL SCHOLARSHIP
Marshall Aid Commemoration Commission
John Foster House, ACU
36 Gordon Square
London WC1H 0PF UNITED KINGDOM
E-mail: info@marshallscholarship.org
Web: www.marshallscholarship.org

Marshall Scholarships, established to encourage international exchange between the United Kingdom and the United States, are awarded to U.S. university graduates to study at a British university for two years. Graduates can apply through the British Consulate for their region. A list of consulate offices is available on the website, or contact the commission office listed above.

NATIONAL SECURITY EDUCATION PROGRAM
UNDERGRADUATE SCHOLARSHIPS
Institute of International Education
1400 K Street NW, 6th Floor
Washington, DC 20005 USA
Tel: (800) 618-NSEP or (202) 326-7697
Fax: (202) 326-7698

E-mail: nsep@iie.org
Web: www.iie.org/nsep

NATIONAL SECURITY EDUCATION PROGRAM GRADUATE SCHOLARSHIPS
Academy for Educational Development
1825 Connecticut Avenue NW
Washington, DC 20009 USA
Tel: (800) 498-9360 or (202) 884-8285
Fax: (202) 884-8407
E-mail: nsep@aed.org
Web: http://nsep.aed.org

National Security Education Program provides scholarship and fellowship funding for undergraduate and graduate students from the United States who wish to study in the field of international affairs and national security. Recipients use the funding for participation in a qualifying study abroad program.

PEACE CORPS
1111 20th Street NW
Washington, DC 20526 USA
Tel: (800) 424-8580
TTY: (202) 692-1857
Web: www.peacecorps.gov

The Peace Corps has thousands of U.S. volunteers serving in more than 70 countries. Volunteers work in the areas of agriculture, appropriate technology, economic development, education, the environment, fisheries, forestry, health and youth development. Peace Corps Volunteers serve for two years, in addition to a 9-12 week training program, and receive a stipend to cover expenses abroad.

ROTARY INTERNATIONAL
One Rotary Center
1560 Sherman Avenue
Evanston, IL 60201 USA
Tel: (847) 866-3000
Fax: (847) 328-8554 or (847) 328-8281
E-mail: rotary@rotary.org
Web: www.rotary.org

Exchange programs for both U.S. and non-U.S. citizens include: Rotary Foundation Ambassadorial Scholarships Program for students, Rotary Foundation Group Study Exchange Program for young professionals, and Rotary Grants for University Teachers to Serve in Developing Countries.

SCHOOL FOR FIELD STUDIES
10 Federal Street
Salem, MA 01970 USA
Tel: (800) 989-4418 or (978) 741-3567
Fax: (978) 741-3551
E-mail: admissions@fieldstudies.org
Web: www.fieldstudies.org

School for Field Studies provides high school and college students summer and semester field-study programs overseas. Programs are focused on the environment, including endangered marine mammals studies, fisheries management, sustainable resource options and more.

THOMAS J. WATSON FOUNDATION
293 South Main Street
Providence, RI 02903 USA
Tel: (401) 274-1952
Fax: (401) 274-1954

E-mail: TJW@WatsonFellowship.org
Web: www.watsonfellowship.org

Thomas J. Watson Foundation provides fellowships to graduating seniors from select colleges and universities in the United States to engage in a year of independent study and travel abroad following their graduation. The project must be one that can be pursued with independence and adaptability, and it cannot involve formal study at a foreign institution. It must involve travel to areas where the student has not previously lived or studied for a significant length of time.

UNITED STATES DEPARTMENT OF STATE

Bureau of Educational and Cultural Affairs
301 4th Street SW, Room 234
Washington, DC 20547 USA
Tel: (202) 619-4360
Fax: (202) 401-5914
E-mail: academic@state.gov
Web: http://exchanges.state.gov

The Bureau's Office of Academic Programs manages a wide spectrum of educational exchange programs. Principal among them is the world renowned Fulbright Program, which awards more than 5000 grants annually to U.S. citizens to study, teach, lecture or conduct research abroad, and to foreign citizens to conduct like activities in the United States. The Benjamin Gilman scholarship program provides grants for U.S. undergraduates to study abroad, specifically targeting students with financial need. The Hubert Humphrey Fellowship Program provides academic study and internship opportunities in the United States for mid-career professionals from developing countries in a variety of fields.

Information on these and many other programs may be found on the website listed above. Non-U.S. citizens should contact the

Public Affairs Section of the U.S. Embassy in your country or the EducationUSA office affiliated with it. To locate the U.S. Embassy near you, you may visit the United States embassy website (http://usembassy.state.gov) and link to the embassy in your country. A list of EducationUSA offices is available online at http://educationusa.state.gov/centers.htm.

WILLING WORKERS ON ORGANIC FARMS
PO Box 2675
Lewes BN7 1RB UNITED KINGDOM
hello@wwoof.org.uk
Web: www.wwoof.org

Willing Workers on Organic Farms (WWOOF) provides an opportunity to work on a farm in exchange for room and board. National WWOOF organizations are established in 21 countries and additional placements in other countries are available through farmers willing to take on members of WWOOF.

Websites on International Exchange Programs

ABOUTJOBS.COM
Web: www.aboutjobs.com

Offers information on overseas jobs, summer jobs, resort jobs and internships. Resume postings are also accepted.

ENGLISH LANGUAGE PROGRAMS
www.languageschoolsguide.com
www.aaiep.org
www.uciep.org

Links to English language programs in the United States.

GOABROAD.COM
Web: www.goabroad.com

Offers searchable databases of work, study, volunteer and teaching abroad opportunities, and tips for exchange participants in each of these categories.

IDEALIST
Web: www.idealist.org

Lists a bank of employment, internship and volunteer opportunities all over the world.

INSTITUTE OF INTERNATIONAL EDUCATION
Web: www.iiepassport.org

Offers a searchable database of academic, language, internship and professional programs abroad.

INTERNATIONAL VOLUNTEER PROGRAMS ASSOCIATION
Web: www.volunteerinternational.org

Offers a searchable database of international volunteer programs and volunteer tips.

JOBS AND JOB HUNTING
Web: www.eldis.org/news/jobs.htm

Offers links to employers in the fields of general development, the environment and volunteerism.

PLANETEDU
Web: www.planetedu.com

Offers a searchable database of international opportunities to study, intern, work, volunteer and more.

STUDY IN THE USA
Web: www.studyusa.com

Has links to U.S. English language programs, college and university international programs, boarding schools, summer programs and more.

UNIVERSITY OF CALIFORNIA, IRVINE
Web: www.cie.uci.edu/iop

Provides a comprehensive collection of programs and links to online information.

UNIVERSITY OF MICHIGAN
Web: www.umich.edu/~icenter/overseas/work

Offers links to several sites that feature work and volunteer abroad opportunities.

UNIVERSITY OF MINNESOTA
Web: www.istc.umn.edu

Offers an overview of study, work and travel abroad options.

WORKINGABROAD
Web: www.workingabroad.com

Provides a personalized list of international opportunities to work, volunteer or teach. Requires a small fee.

Publications on International Exchange Programs

ADVISORY LIST
Council on Standards for International Educational Travel (CSIET)
212 South Henry Street

Alexandria, VA 22314 USA
Tel: (703) 739-9050
Fax: (703) 739-9035
E-mail: mailbox@csiet.org
Web: www.csiet.org

The *Advisory List* includes high school international exchange programs that meet the CSIET standards.

ALTERNATIVES TO THE PEACE CORPS
Food First Books
398 60th Street
Oakland, CA 94618 USA
Tel: (510) 654-4400
Fax: (510) 654-4551
E-mail: cdrake@foodfirst.org
Web: www.foodfirst.org

Alternatives to the Peace Corps, edited by Joan Powell, is a guide to voluntary service programs, study abroad opportunities and alternative travel in developing countries. The publication includes a resource guide and bibliography.

THE BACK DOOR GUIDE TO SHORT TERM JOB ADVENTURES
Attention: Michael Landes
158 Walnut Road
Lake Peekskill, NY 10537 USA
Tel: (914) 260-7919
E-mail: mlandes@backdoorjobs.com
Web: www.backdoorjobs.com

The Back Door Guide to Short Term Job Adventures is an international guide to paid internships, seasonal jobs, volunteer opportunities and work abroad.

DIRECTORY OF INTERNATIONAL INTERNSHIPS: A WORLD OF OPPORTUNITIES

Michigan State University
Instructional Media Center
PO Box 710
East Lansing, MI 48824 USA
Tel: (517) 353-9229
Fax: (517) 432-2650
E-mail: gliozzo@pilot.msu.edu
Web: www.isp.msu.edu/InternationalInternships/index.html

Directory of International Internships: A World of Opportunities lists a wide variety of experiential educational opportunities abroad, for academic credit, pay or just for experience.

THE GLOBAL CITIZEN

Ten Speed Press
PO Box 7123
Berkeley, CA 94707 USA
Tel: (800) 841-2665 or (510) 559-1600
Fax: (510) 559-1629
E-mail: order@tenspeed.com
Web: www.tenspeed.com

The Global Citizen, by Elizabeth Kruempelmann, is a guide to creating an international life and career for you and even your family whether you are a student, professional or retiree. It includes tips on planning an exchange experience as well as listings of programs and resources.

GLOBAL WORK

InterAction Publications Department
1717 Massachusetts Avenue NW, Suite 701
Washington, DC 20036 USA

Tel: (202) 667-8227
Fax: (202) 667-8236
E-mail: publications@interaction.org
Web: www.interaction.org

Global Work, published by InterAction, is a directory of international internship and volunteer opportunities in the development field.

INSTITUTE OF INTERNATIONAL EDUCATION
IIE Books
E-mail: iiebooks@pmds.com
Web: www.iiebooks.org

The Institute of International Education publishes *Academic Year Abroad* and *Short-Term Study Abroad* for study and internship programs overseas, and *Intensive English USA,* which lists English language programs.

INTERNATIONAL EXCHANGE LOCATOR
Alliance for International Educational and Cultural Exchange
1776 Massachusetts Avenue NW, Suite 620
Washington, DC 20036 USA
Tel: (888) 304-9023 or (202) 293-6141
Fax: (202) 293-6144
E-mail: info@alliance-exchange.org
Web: www.alliance-exchange.org

The *International Exchange Locator*, produced by the Alliance for International Educational and Cultural Exchange with support from the U.S. Department of State, includes information on international exchange organizations and programs worldwide. The directory includes profiles on nonprofit organizations, exchanges offered throughout 35 U.S. federal agencies, a comprehensive listing of the U.S. Department of State's offices involved in exchange programs, and specific program overviews of exchange organizations.

INVEST YOURSELF: THE CATALOGUE OF VOLUNTEER OPPORTUNITIES

Commission on Voluntary Service and Action
PO Box 117
New York, NY 10009 USA
Tel: (800) 356-9315 or (718) 638-8487
Fax: (718) 638-8487

Invest Yourself is a guide to action for those looking for non-governmental volunteer opportunities in the United States and around the world.

PETERSON'S GUIDES

2000 Lenox Drive
Lawrenceville, NJ 08648 USA
Tel: (800) 338-3282 or (609) 896-1800 ext. 3435
Fax: (609) 896-1811
E-mail: custsvc@petersons.com
Web: www.petersons.com

Peterson's Guides publishes several work abroad resource books. *Directory of Overseas Summer Jobs* lists more than 50,000 jobs worldwide, *Summer Opportunities for Kids and Teenagers* has a variety of camps, exchanges and projects worldwide and *Colleges and Universities in the USA* and *Internships* are for those planning to study or intern in the United States.

TRANSITIONS ABROAD PUBLISHING

PO Box 745
Bennington, VT 05201 USA
Tel/Fax: (802) 442-4827
E-mail: info@transitionsabroad.com
Web: www.transitionsabroad.com

Transitions Abroad publishes a magazine and a number of useful books: *Work Abroad: The Complete Guide to Finding a Job Overseas* and *Alternative Travel Directory: The Complete Guide to Work, Study, Travel Overseas.* All are useful for individuals interested in going abroad to travel, study, volunteer, teach, work or do an internship.

VACATION WORK PUBLICATIONS
9 Park End Street
Oxford, OX1 1HJ ENGLAND
Tel: (44-1865) 241-978
E-mail: sales@vacationwork.co.uk
Web: www.vacationwork.co.uk

International Directory of Voluntary Work, Work Your Way Around the World, and *Teaching English Abroad* profile hundreds of organizations seeking skilled and unskilled volunteers, teachers, and seasonal workers or other short-term job seekers.

VOLUNTEER VACATIONS: SHORT-TERM ADVENTURES THAT WILL BENEFIT YOU AND OTHERS
Chicago Review Press
c/o Independent Publishers Group
814 North Franklin Street
Chicago, IL 60610 USA
Tel: (800) 888-4741 or (312) 337-0747
Fax: (312) 337-5985
E-mail: orders@ipgbook.com
Web: www.ipgbook.com

Volunteer Vacations: Short-Term Adventures That Will Benefit You and Others presents more than 500 opportunities for combining holidays and adventure in the United States and other countries, including opportunities for volunteering internationally.

Disability Organizations

The following are those U.S.-based and international disability-related organizations mentioned throughout this publication. For more organizations, visit the National Clearinghouse on Disability and Exchange / Mobility International USA website at www.miusa.org to browse the disability organizations worldwide searchable database, the resource sheets on the publications page and the links page.

AMERICAN FEDERATION OF THE BLIND
11 Penn Plaza, Suite 300
New York, NY 10001 USA
Tel: (800) 232-5463 or (212) 502-7600
Fax: (212) 502-7777
E-mail: afbinfo@afb.org
Web: www.afb.org

The American Foundation for the Blind (AFB) is a national non-profit serving as a resource for people who are blind or visually impaired, the organizations that serve them, and the general public. AFB offers information and referral services, produces a wide-range of resources, and provides several scholarships to students who are legally blind or visually impaired.

DISABLED PEOPLES' INTERNATIONAL
748 Broadway
Winnipeg, Manitoba R3G 0X3 CANADA
Tel: (204) 287-8010
Fax: (204) 783-6270
E-mail: info@dpi.org
Web: www.dpi.org

Disabled Peoples' International's (DPI) purpose is to extend the principles of human rights to all people with disabilities, including the right to full participation in their families, their communities, their nations and in all spheres of their lives. DPI is involved in promoting and lobbying for the human rights of disabled people at the international level, and has affiliates worldwide.

DISABILITY RADIO WORLDWIDE
PO Box 200567
Denver, CO 80220 USA
Tel: (303) 355-9935
Fax: (303) 316-7789
E-mail: global3@concentric.net
Web: www.independentliving.org/radio

Disability Radio Worldwide is a weekly half hour radio program that is broadcast on the Internet at www.acbradio.org. The show is broadcast to over 100 countries on short-wave frequencies 6975, 15050 and 21460. The program includes interviews with people with various disabilities covering a variety of topics, such as reproductive health care, women with disabilities and the progress of children with disabilities in developing countries.

DISABILITY RIGHTS EDUCATION AND DEFENSE FUND
2212 Sixth Street
Berkeley, CA 94710 USA
Tel/TTY: (510) 644-2555
Fax: (510) 841-8645
E-mail: dredf@dredf.org
Web: www.dredf.org

The Disability Rights Education and Defense Fund (DREDF) is a national, nonprofit law and policy center, dedicated to furthering the civil rights of people with disabilities. DREDF provides technical assistance, information and referral, and training to individuals and organizations on disability-rights laws and policies, and provides legal representation directly and as co-counsel and amicus in cases of disability-based discrimination. DREDF has organized international symposia, conducted overseas trainings and contributed to a book on international disability laws and policies.

INCLUSION INTERNATIONAL
115 Golden Lane
London EC1Y 0TJ UNITED KINGDOM
Tel: (44-207) 696-6904
Fax: (44-207) 696-5589
E-mail: info@inclusion-international.org
Web: www.inclusion-international.org

Inclusion International is a grassroots organization of families, self-advocates and committed citizens with a focus on advocacy. Founded in 1960, this organization protects the human rights of people with mental disabilities.

INTERNATIONAL RESCUE COMMITTEE
122 East 42nd Street
New York, NY 10168 USA
Tel: (212) 551-3000
Fax: (212) 551-3184
E-mail: info@theirc.org
Web: www.theirc.org

International Rescue Committee (IRC) provides emergency relief, public health, medical and educational services to refugees and displaced people abroad. Through reconstruction and rehabilitation projects, IRC assists in the repatriation of refugees to their home countries, provides resettlement services for refugees in the United States and advocates on behalf of refugees, especially women and children.

PARALYZED VETERANS OF AMERICA

801 Eighteenth Street NW
Washington, DC 20006 USA
Tel: (800) 424-8200 or (202) 872-1300
TTY: (202) 416-7622
Fax: (202) 785-4452
E-mail: info@pva.org
Web: www.pva.org

Paralyzed Veterans of America administers programs in advocacy, sports and recreation, spinal cord injury treatment research, legislative lobbying, transportation (including air travel), employment and disability rights. Its website contains a variety of useful, downloadable disability-related resources.

REHABILITATION INTERNATIONAL

25 East 21st Street
New York, NY 10010 USA
Tel: (212) 420-1500
TTY: (212) 420-1752
Fax: (212) 505-0871
E-mail: rehabintl@rehab-international.org
Web: www.rehab-international.org

Rehabilitation International (RI) is an organization that works to promote the prevention of disability, the rehabilitation of disabled people and the equalization of opportunities for people with disabilities. RI publishes an array of periodicals and reports on disability issues. Its website lists membership organizations worldwide.

SUPPORT COALITION INTERNATIONAL

PO Box 11284
Eugene, OR 97440 USA

Tel: (877) 623-7743 or (541) 345-9106
Fax: (541) 345-3737
E-mail: office@MindFreedom.org
Web: www.MindFreedom.org

Support Coalition International is an international coalition of groups that advocate for human rights in psychiatry, and includes current and former mental health consumers. They can provide information on support and advocacy groups abroad in several countries.

WORLD BLIND UNION
José Ortega y Gasset 22-24, 4°
28006 Madrid SPAIN
Tel: (34-91) 589-4533 or (34-91) 589-4692
Fax: (34-91) 589-4749
E-mail: umc@once.es
Web: www.worldblindunion.org

World Blind Union focuses on human rights and equal opportunities for blind and visually impaired people worldwide. Its website lists worldwide members.

WORLD FEDERATION OF THE DEAF
PO Box 65
00401 Helsinki FINLAND
TTY: (358-9) 580-3573
Fax: (358-9) 580-3572
E-mail: info@wfdnews.org
Web: www.wfdnews.org

World Federation of the Deaf is an international, non-governmental organization of national associations of Deaf people. A list of over 100 member organizations worldwide is available on the website.

WORLD INSTITUTE ON DISABILITY

510 16th Street, Suite 100

Oakland, CA 94612 USA

Tel: (510) 763-4100

TTY: (510) 208-9496

Fax: (510) 763-4109

E-mail: info@wid.org

Web: www.wid.org

World Institute on Disability (WID) is a center for the development of public policy that promotes the civil rights, health, well-being and independence of people with disabilities. WID provides training (including an internship) for people from around the world who are interested in the independent living movement. WID also has an online magazine that focuses on international disability topics.

WORLD NETWORK OF USERS AND SURVIVORS OF PSYCHIATRY

Secretariat

Klingenberg 15, 2.th

5000 Odense C, DENMARK

Tel: (45) 6619-4511

E-mail: admin@wnusp.org

Web: www.wnusp.org

World Network of Users and Survivors of Psychiatry provides a global forum and voice for users and survivors of psychiatry to promote their rights and interests. The organization includes people with psychiatric disabilities and professionals interested in furthering human rights in psychiatry.

Travel Services and Information for People with Disabilities

ACCESS-ABLE

Web: www.access-able.com

This travel agency's website provides extensive access information for mature and disabled travelers.

AVIATION CONSUMER PROTECTION DIVISION

Web: http://airconsumer.ost.dot.gov

This U.S. Department of Transportation website has fact sheets on security and accessibility requirements for air travel.

DISABLED TRAVEL NETWORK

Web: www.geocities.com/Paris/1502/

This website allows readers to exchange travel information and experiences.

EMERGING HORIZONS

Web: www.emerginghorizons.com

This organization provides accessible travel resources, such as *Barrier-Free Travel: A Nuts & Bolts Guide for Wheelers and Slow Walkers.*

GIMP ON THE GO

Web: www.gimponthego.com

This online travel publication offers people with disabilities feature articles, resource listings, and readers' comments.

MOSS REHAB RESOURCE NET

Web: www.mossresourcenet.org

A list of additional travel resources for people with disabilities are linked off of this website.

Lodging

ACCESSIBLE VACATION HOME EXCHANGE
Web: www.independentliving.org/vacex

This free, web-based global service allows homeowners to post information about their accessible houses, apartments and condominiums, and to contact each other to arrange housing exchanges.

HOSTELLING INTERNATIONAL
International Youth Hostel Federation
1st Floor, Fountain House, Parkway
Welwyn Garden City
Herts AL8 6JH UNITED KINGDOM
Tel: (44-1707) 324-170
Fax: (44-1707) 323-980
Web: www.iyhf.org

This international lodging network allows travelers to stay inexpensively in cities around the world. Kitchen facilities and single occupancy to dormitory style rooms are provided, as well as other amenities such as cafes, internet and travel information depending on the location. Some accessibility information is provided in the descriptions of each hostel.

UNITED STATES SERVAS, INC.
11 John Street, Room 505
New York, NY 10038 USA
Tel: (212) 267-0252

Fax: (212) 267-0292
E-mail: info@usservas.org
Web: www.usservas.org

This international, non-governmental organization connects international travelers, including people with disabilities, with hosts in various parts of the world.

Health Resources

AMERICAN ASSOCIATION OF KIDNEY PATIENTS
3505 East Frontage Road, Suite 315
Tampa, FL 33607 USA
Tel: (800) 749-2257 or (813) 636-8100
Fax: (813) 636-8122
E-mail: info@aakp.org
Web: www.aakp.org

American Association of Kidney Patients provides a variety of resources for people who use dialysis.

AMERICAN DIABETES ASSOCIATION
1701 North Beauregard Street
Alexandria, VA 22311 USA
Tel: (800) 342-2383
Fax: (703) 549-6995
E-mail: AskADA@diabetes.org
Web: www.diabetes.org

The American Diabetes Association has tips and advice about traveling with diabetes, including pre-trip preparations, crossing time zones, air travel with diabetes supplies, etc.

CENTERS FOR DISEASE CONTROL AND PREVENTION

Tel: (877) 394-8747
Fax: (888) 232-3299
Web: www.cdc.gov/travel

The Centers for Disease Control and Prevention maintains health-related information online, including travel preparation and health information for travel worldwide.

HESPERIAN FOUNDATION

1919 Addison Street, Suite 304
Berkeley, CA 94704 USA
Tel: (888) 729-1796 or (510) 845-1447
Fax: (510) 845-9141
E-mail: hesperian@hesperian.org
Web: www.hesperian.org

This non-profit organization publishes books to enable people to take care of their own healthcare, such as *Where There is No Doctor* or *Disabled Village Children.*

INTERNATIONAL ASSOCIATION FOR MEDICAL ASSISTANCE TO TRAVELERS

417 Center Street
Lewiston, NY 14092 USA
Tel: (716) 754-4883
E-mail: info@iamat.org
Web: www.iamat.org

This organization provides a directory of English-speaking doctors in 500 cities in 120 countries, and other health information as well.

RESOURCE DIRECTORY FOR VENTILATOR-ASSISTED LIVING

Post Polio Health International

4207 Lindell Boulevard, Suite 110
Saint Louis, MO 63108 USA
Tel: (314) 534-0475
Fax: (314) 534-5070
E-mail: info@post-polio.org
Web: www.post-polio.org

This directory is published annually and includes sections on health professionals and ventilator users experienced in and committed to living independently at home with a ventilator; ventilator equipment manufacturers; ventilator service and repair companies; face and nasal mask manufacturers; and non-profit organizations, foundations and associations worldwide.

PERSONALMD

4725 First Street, Suite 275
Pleasanton, CA 94566 USA
Tel: (925) 417-6840
Fax: (925) 600-7568
Web: www.PersonalMD.com

This consumer health website provides information on a wide variety of topics pertaining to health. It also provides information on obtaining its PersonalMD Emergency Card. At no cost, cardholders may enter their medical information into a secure database that can be accessed anywhere in the world via the Internet if there is an emergency.

SHORELAND'S TRAVEL HEALTH ONLINE

Web: www.tripprep.com

This website provides travelers' health information, a planning guide and country information.

Intercultural Communication and International Career Books

In addition to this list, check your local or online bookstores and libraries for travel guides and travelers' tales for the country you are traveling to.

CAREERS IN INTERNATIONAL AFFAIRS
Georgetown University Press
3240 Prospect Street NW
Washington, DC 20007 USA
Tel: (202) 687-5889
Fax: (202) 687-6340
E-mail: gupress@georgetown.edu
Web: http://press.georgetown.edu

Careers in International Affairs, edited by Maria Pinto Carland and Michael Trucano at the Georgetown University School of Foreign Service, provides essays on international careers and organizational profiles that detail qualifications for positions and availability of internships.

CAREERS IN INTERNATIONAL EDUCATION, EXCHANGE, AND DEVELOPMENT
NAFSA Publications
PO Box 1020
Sewickly, PA 15143 USA
Tel: (800) 836-4994 or (412) 741-1142
Fax: (412) 741-0609
E-mail: publications@nafsa.org
Web: www.nafsa.org

Careers in International Education, Exchange, and Development outlines tips and resources for those beginning or continuing a career in the international education, exchange and development fields.

CULTUREGRAMS
333 South 520 West, Suite 360
Lindon, UT 84042 USA
Tel: (800) 528-6279 or (801) 932-6440
Fax: (801) 847-0127
E-mail: support@culturegrams.com
Web: www.culturegrams.com

CultureGrams provide brief descriptions of the culture, geography, history, language, politics and other information about countries worldwide.

IMPACT PUBLICATIONS
9104 Manassas Drive, Suite N
Manassas Park, VA 20111 USA
Tel: (800) 361-1055 or (703) 361-7300
Fax: (703) 335-9486
E-mail: info@impactpublications.com
Web: www.impactpublications.com

A wide variety of books on international exchange, finding a job overseas and cross-cultural issues are available from Impact Publications.

INTERCULTURAL PRESS
374 US Route One
Yarmouth, ME 04096 USA
Tel: (866) 372-2665 or (207) 846-5168
Fax: (207) 846-5181
E-mail: books@interculturalpress.com
Web: www.interculturalpress.com

This publisher carries a variety of books and resources useful for those interested in intercultural communication, international education and exchange.

Index

A

Aaron, Jessica, 29–30, 135–136, 154
Abbott, Rachel, 68–69, 156–158
academic opportunities abroad, 23
access barriers abroad, 116–117
Accessible Home Swap, 67–68
accommodations and accessibility
    arranging, 75–78
    creating your own, 143
    disclosing your disability, 39–43
    encountering discrimination,
      40–41
    forming a support team, 145
    handling housing issues, 146–150
    requesting disability-related ac-
      commodations, 43–44, 143–144
    school, 144–146
    transferability of accommodations,
      141–142
    workplace, 142–143
ADA, *see* Americans with Disabilities
    Act
Adams, Cheryl, 24
Africa, 4, 97, 115, 136, 138

AFS Intercultural Programs, 146
Air Carriers Access Act (ACAA),
    107–108
air travel, 105–110, 201
Allard, Angie, 20–21
alliances and friendships, 154
American Sign Language (ASL), 77,
    84–85, 146
Americans with Disabilities Act
    (ADA), 3–4, 14, 40
anxieties about traveling, coping with,
    30, 74
Arellano, Leticia, 149, 163
arthritis, 108
Asia, 4, 69, 137, 183
ASL, *see* American Sign Language
assistance
    planning for, 82–90
    requesting, 112–114
    unwanted, 115
Augsburg College, Center for Global
    Education at, 8
Australia, 11, 92
Aviation Consumer Protection
    Division, 201